Domestic Satellite:
An FCC Giant Step

Westview Replica Editions

This book is a Westview Replica Edition. The concept of Replica Editions is a response to the crisis in academic and informational publishing. Library budgets for books have been severely curtailed; economic pressures on the university presses and the few private publishing companies primarily interested in scholarly manuscripts have severely limited the capacity of the industry to properly serve the academic and research communities. Many manuscripts dealing with important subjects, often representing the highest level of scholarship, are today not economically viable publishing projects. Or, if they are accepted for publication, they are often subject to lead times ranging from one to three years. Scholars are understandably frustrated when they realize that their first-class research cannot be published within a reasonable time frame, if at all.

Westview Replica Editions seem to us one feasible and practical solution to the crisis. The concept is simple. We accept a manuscript in camera-ready form and move it immediately into the production process. The responsibility for textual and copy editing lies with the author or sponsoring organization. If necessary we will advise the author on proper preparation of footnotes and bibliography. The manuscript is acceptable as typed for a thesis or dissertation or prepared in any other clearly organized and readable way, though we prefer it typed according to our specifications. The end result is a book produced by lithography and bound in hard covers. Edition sizes range from 200 to 600 copies. We will include among Westview Replica Editions only works of outstanding scholarly quality or of great informational value and we will exercise our usual editorial standards and quality control.

Domestic Satellite: An FCC Giant Step
Toward Competitive Telecommunications Policy

Robert S. Magnant

In a society where as much as 50 percent of the gross national product is spent on information transfer services, trends in communications policy and capabilities become extremely important and can have major consequences. During the past ten years, the Federal Communications Commission has made a major effort to promote competition and innovation in the telecommunications industry. But, in order that public interests be identified and adequately served, there must be a wider understanding of the industry and the issues. Robert Magnant takes full account of the multidisciplinary nature of the telecommunications field, and in this book presents an objective treatment of technological trends, policy issues, and market constraints. His study has been designed to provide intelligible, easily accessible information for the legislator, the business leader, the concerned citizen. It deals with the specific area of telecommunications, but in its complete coverage of a major domestic policy issue, it is at the same time an excellent case study to illuminate the intricacies and options in the formulation and operation both of general government and business policy and, more specifically, regulated market structures.

Robert S. Magnant is chief engineer and technical director for the U.S. Army Communications Electronics Engineering Installation Agency—Continental United States (USACEEIA-CONUS). In 1976, while on academic leave from his position with USACEEIA, he received a master's degree in telecommunications from the University of Colorado.

Domestic Satellite: An FCC Giant Step

Toward Competitive Telecommunications Policy

Robert S. Magnant

Westview Press
Boulder, Colorado

A Westview Replica Edition

Published 1977 in the United States of America by
    Westview Press, Inc.
    1898 Flatiron Court
    Boulder, Colorado 80301
    Frederick A. Praeger, Publisher and Editorial Director

Library of Congress Cataloging in Publication Data

Magnant, Robert S.
    Domestic satellite.

    (A Westview replica edition)
    Bibliography: p.
    1. United States. Federal Telecommunications Commission.
    2. Artificial satellites in telecommunication. I. Title.
HE9721.U5M33 1977   384.54'56   76-30840
ISBN 0-89158-226-6

Printed and bound in the United States of America

To the memory of Eric W. Muller, Jr. --

        a true professional and a very dear friend.

TABLE OF CONTENTS

TABLE OF CONTENTS (continued)

TABLE OF CONTENTS (continued)

LIST OF TABLES

LIST OF ILLUSTRATIONS

PREFACE

The Federal Communications Commission is the licensing and regulatory authority for the private, nongovernmental interstate and foreign telecommunications of the United States. Consequently its activities affect virtually everyone either directly or indirectly. Since its establishment by Congressional legislation in 1934, its activities, its personalities and its policies have occasionally been the object of lengthy discussion and debate; however, its role during the past ten years has been particularly controversial.

Instead of merely interpreting existing law, the Commission, by necessity, must continually break new ground in order to accommodate new uses of communications technology as was exemplified by its decisions in the application of satellites to domestic communications and the interdependence of computers and communications. In addition, since 1959, the Commission has promoted a definite policy of increased competition in the industry. Such groundbreaking efforts are now manifesting themselves in the current filing before the Commission of Satellite Business Systems [an IBM sponsored partnership] for a wideband, digitized domestic satellite system.

A review of the factors that have influenced
the Commission's domestic satellite policy provides a
picture of the increasingly complex world of this
Federal regulatory agency. The main hypothesis of
this study is that this policy was a profound decision
by the Commission [possibly the most important and
most complex in the Commission's history] with a
lasting potential for benefit to the public inherent
in it. The significant points of technology and policy
raised by the SBS filing are discussed to show the
potential of SBS to offer innovative services to data
communications users and to compete with the communication industry's dominant monopoly, American Telephone
and Telegraph.

This subject is considered to be an excellent
example of interdisciplinary interactions in the field
of telecommunications. An appreciation for such
interactions is generally necessary when addressing
any telecommunication issue. It is intended that this
study will give added emphasis to the merging of
computer and communications technologies and promote
an increased appreciation for satellite regulation at
both the national and international levels.

ACKNOWLEDGMENTS

The following pages are dedicated to Professionals; people of the highest standards--like Geoffrey Ballard, Les Callahan, Irwin Higgs, Bill Kenneally, W. B. Latta, Norman Shupe, and the members of the U.S. Army's Communications-Electronics Engineering Installation Agency--as well as many others whom I have either known or worked with within the Department of the Army over the past twelve years. These are motivated, hard-working people who believe in what they are doing. There are such people within the Federal Communications Commission.

Sy Greenspan and Harold Randall deserve particular note for having done more than their fair share; guiding me, teaching me (with much patience I might add), believing in me, and consequently making this year and this work possible. The support of my wife, Rosemary, goes without saying.

Special appreciation is extended to Dr. George A. Codding, Jr., Dr. Frank S. Barnes and the University of Colorado faculty for their guidance and assistance in the development of this effort. Jim Alleman and the members of the Policy Research Division staff at the Department of Commerce, Office of Telecommunications, have contributed valuable commentary to me throughout this study and I am particularly indebted to Cheryl Zegers, Technical Information Specialist at the Department of Commerce's Boulder Library, for her data-gathering assistance.

The information and support contributed to this effort by the individuals listed in Appendix A through interviews and/or correspondence and documentation will never be fully quantified. I wish to also thank Dick Talley of Hughes Aircraft for his critique of the draft manuscript and Dale Hatfield and Seb Lasher of the Federal Communications Commission for their comments and criticisms of this effort.

Any viewpoints found in the text without citations are those of the author and should not be construed as the opinions or the official interpretations of policy of the individuals or organizations discussed.

R.S.M.

Boulder, Colorado
July, 1976

INTRODUCTION

In deference to Arthur Clark and Marshall
McLuhan, this study begins with neither a quote from
"Extraterrestrial Relays" nor a profound discussion
of the satellite's molding of the human race into a
global village.[1] The existence of communications
satellites is as second nature to the bicentennial
American as moon landings. The "LIVE VIA SATELLITE"
caption at the bottom of a television picture (if
it's even indicated anymore) no longer gives special
cause for notice or excitement. Today, without
having direct involvement in either the aerospace
or telecommunications industry, the average individual
could easily conclude that the "communications by
satellite" revolution was a product of the 60's and
think no more of it. In fact, satellite technology
has had and continues to have a major impact on the
capabilities of today's world-wide telecommunication
systems. Its applications to domestic communications
are just beginning to be developed and several options

---

[1]Clark's 1945 article, predicting the use of
synchronous satellites for communication, appears in
the Appendix of his Voices from the Sky (New York:
Harper and Row, 1965). Also see Neil P. Hurley,
"Marshall McLuhan: Communications Explorer," The
McLuhan Explosion, H. H. Crosby and G. R. Bond, eds.
(New York: The American Book Company, 1968), pp. 154-59.

are either in the proposal stage or being implemented.

Telecommunications has been defined by the International Telecommunication Union as:

> Any transmission, emission or reception
> of signs, signals, writing images and
> sound or intelligence of any nature by
> wire, radio, optical, or other electro-
> magnetic systems.

Unfortunately, there are many people who are unaware of this definition, or any simpler definition for that matter, of what telecommunications is and what it means to their individual lives. Complicating any understanding of telecommunications are the economic considerations of regulated and competitive markets. The United States, traditionally a competitive, free-enterprise market, is one of the few countries of the world where telecommunications is part of the private sector, as opposed to national systems. Private concerns furnish communications services to the nation that are "affected with a public interest." Conse-quently these firms are designated as "public utilities" and from an economic standpoint, they possess techno-logical characteristics that almost inevitably result in monopoly market structures. American Telephone and Telegraph (AT&T) has long dominated this nation's communications market.

Generally, it is agreed that where the common benefit is dominant, where the whole of society is involved, economic functions will be performed by society itself. Further, where the common interest requires interference with private functions, government will intervene. Public utilities and similar regulated industries are a "halfway house" between completely government functions and free enterprise functions.[2] Regulation is imposed by the government to fix reasonable prices for the services rendered as a substitute for competition. Under the present structure, the Federal Communications Commission (FCC) is the government body having primary responsibility for regulatory policy in the telecommunications area.

In domestic telecommunications, a changing market structure and a pervasive rate of technical innovation have fostered a dynamic regulatory environment. Since 1959 the communications common carrier industry has been undergoing a transition as a result of several new policies that have been instituted by the FCC to promote competition in the industry. Also the rapid rate of technological innovation of the 1960's has blended, if not merged, the computer and communications technologies together. One of the Commission's more recent policies, Domestic Satellite, stands out as unique and seems to be the embodiment of all the pro-competitive policies of the FCC to date.

---

[2]Martin T. Farris and Roy J. Sampson, Public Utilities: Regulation, Management and Ownership (Boston, Massachusetts: Houghton Mifflin Company, 1973), pp. 6-8.

4

The fact that the common carrier industry is a traditionally regulated industry makes this policy and the Commission's role as regulator only more important.

It has been suggested by Adams and Dirlam that nothing could better illustrate the pressures that a regulatory commission must resist [in the execution of its duties during periods of dynamic technological change] than the satellite.[3] On March 2, 1966 the Commission formally initiated a Notice of Inquiry, Docket No. 16495--In the Matter of Establishment of Domestic Noncommon Carrier Communications Satellite Facilities by Nongovernmental Entities, but it was over six years later before it finalized a "limited open entry" policy for domestic communications satellites. Through a review of official documents, literature searches, formal correspondence and personal interviews, this research examines the factors which appear to have influenced the Commission's Domestic Satellite [also to be referred to as DOMSAT] proceedings and identifies present considerations that have been placed before the Commission since that ruling. Such analysis:

(1) provides a comprehensive picture of the multi-faceted interface that the FCC has with its

_____

[3]Walter Adams, Joel B. Dirlam, "Market Structure, Regulation, and Dynamic Change," Performance Under Regulation, Harry M. Trebing, ed. (East Lansing, Michigan: MSU Public Utilities Studies, 1968), pp. 131-144.

environment,

(2) demonstrates how interrelated the issues can become when determining policy in an area of dynamic technological change,

(3) shows how the inherent technical characteristics of communications satellites [which have no exact terrestrial equivalent] and the advances in computer-communications have contributed to the complexity of this issue, and

(4) identifies instances where the satellite policies of four different presidential administrations, compounded with an assortment of study groups, personalities, industry postures and international considerations confounded the issue before the Commission.

The objective of this study is that it serve as a vehicle for increasing the "public's awareness" to the subject of telecommunications and to the status of the domestic satellite issue and, as a consequence, lend support to the Commission in its current and future efforts. The FCC's performance in the regulation of today's common carriers has not been receiving the respect it deserves. However, confidence in the Commission's capabilities and the effectiveness of the regulatory process is central to the public and national interest.[4]

---

[4]Final Report, President's Task Force on Communications Policy, December 7, 1968 (Washington, D.C.: U.S. Government Printing Office, 1969), 0-351-636, Tab B, p. 9.

The FCC comprises men and women, professionals in their fields, who are attempting to perform an enormous task with limited resources. It is impossible for them to have all the right answers all the time in such a complex world as theirs. Even Sir Arthur Clark, looking back on the proposition of patenting his 1945 concept, notes:

> The idea of patenting the geostationary communications satellite concept never occurred to me and my excuse for this is sheer lack of imagination.[5]

This study offers a positive perspective of Commission's efforts in an area of dynamic technology. The adequacy of the FCC's organizational structure is not an issue but rather a factor which is addressed in passing only.

The analysis of the Commission's domestic satellite considerations is arranged to follow the historical pattern of events surrounding DOMSAT. The problem, however, is initially set within the framework of the business considerations and the technical limitations that existed. The time value of such information played an important role in the policy-making process. Time controls the available technology, it defines the existing and projected business markets and it determines the political

---

[5]Arthur Clark, Voices from the Sky (New York: Harper and Row, 1965), p. 125.

priorities of the day. The emphasis given to each of these factors varied throughout the DOMSAT proceedings.

This study of the policy-making process divides itself into three distinct periods:

(1959-1965) - the precedents of DOMSAT.

(1966-1972) - the development of the DOMSAT policy.

(1973 to present) - DOMSAT policy today.

The logical starting date for this review is 1959 as it was in December of that year that President Eisenhower first spoke of the commercial use of communications satellites. Also 1959 is a well-documented date for the beginning of the FCC's current policy of competition. The initial period of discussion is from 1959 up until the DOMSAT question was raised by the American Broadcasting Company's filing in 1965 and is covered in Chapter II. This period includes the policy precedents of the Eisenhower and Kennedy Administrations that resulted in the Communications Satellite Act of 1962.

Chapter III covers from March 2, 1966, the date of issuance of the Commission's Notice of Inquiry on DOMSAT (Docket No. 16495) through December 22, 1972, the date of the Commission's final Memorandum Opinion and Order. This is the period when formal DOMSAT policy was defined. Chapter IV looks at DOMSAT from then until today, focusing briefly on some of the

results of that decision, and more specifically on the
activity surrounding the filing by Satellite Business
Systems from current business, technical and regulatory
perspectives.

Primary information sources used for this study
were official FCC Notices, Reports, Orders and
Memorandums as well as filings, briefs and comments
submitted by the industries involved in DOMSAT. Official
Congressional documentation was used to a large extent
as was current formal correspondence from the individuals listed in Appendix A. Automated data base
searches were also used for this research and the
opinions and analyses used in the following discussions
are viewpoints taken from the appropriate periods of
time to the greatest extent possible. The formal
correspondence noted served both as primary sources
of information and as guides which provided direction
to the research. Secondary sources of information
were textbooks, journals, newspapers, presentations,
and published reports.

CHAPTER I

HISTORICAL FOUNDATIONS AND
BOUNDARY CONDITIONS

To understand the impact of the <u>Domestic Satellite</u> decision, an understanding of the origins of regulation, the domestic communication common carriers and the Federal Communications Commission is required. The roots of the FCC date back more than fifty years to the early days of radio. The legislation by which Congress established this independent agency to regulate the nation's communications and encourage the larger and more effective use of radio in the public interest remains essentially unchanged today.

The world of the FCC is far from simple. The Commission must interface with its environment in a multitude of ways in the performance of its regulatory functions and without a doubt, the common carriers dominate this interface. Technology and market considerations have shaped the industry's structure but both vary with time and both have imposed constraints on the policy makers and have limited the alternatives for them.

This chapter reviews the foundations of the

organizations and industries that participated in DOMSAT.
These provide the initial conditions (as well as the
constraints) from which a new domestic industry was
launched with initial annual revenue estimated in
excess of one-half billion dollars and initial investment estimates of almost three times that value.[1]
Technology was a major consideration throughout the
DOMSAT proceedings. Thus definitions of the boundaries
which it created will increase the reader's appreciation
for the issues that were before the Commission.
Working definitions of competition, regulation, the
common carriers, the rate base and the public interest
are also provided to establish the baselines that
business considerations imposed on DOMSAT.

A. The Federal Communications Commission
    and the Common Carrier Industry

The one hundredth anniversary of the invention
of the telephone and the beginning of the communications
common carriers is being celebrated this year. In
contrast the FCC is only forty-two years old and
generally considered to be a "late bloomer"; its
effectiveness as a regulator has only been noticeable
during the last two decades. Perhaps this is because
demands for new and different services surfaced during

---

[1]John McDonald, "Getting Our Communication
Satellite Off the Ground," Fortune, 86 (July, 1972),
p. 69.

this period as a result of technological advances.

The improvements in the appearance of a modern
telephone instrument over an antique device are in no
way a measure of the service improvements available.
Today's telecommunications systems, when compared
against yesterday's predictions, are orders of magnitude
greater than the wildest dreams imagined attainable
by our ancestors and they extend far beyond the realm
of voice communications and the traditional common
carriers.

Although the Commission and the common carriers
evolved separately, it is important that their origins
be understood. These perspectives which include
information relative to the Commission's formation,
the roots of the Nation's carriers, the concepts of
regulation, the related legislation and the basic
form of the industry are considered elementary but
necessary background for this study. The carriers,
both old and new, and the FCC are the primary elements
involved in DOMSAT.

1. Regulatory Origins

To operate a broadcasting station in the United
States, one must first obtain a license from the
Federal Communications Commission. The delivery of a
license is not an automatic function but is at the
discretion of the Commission; it is theirs to decide.

How the Commission came to exist and how it acquired
such power is a story that spans the first third of
this century.

Radio was first used commercially for ship-to-
shore and ship-to-ship communication. However, as
early as 1901 low frequency radio began to be used to
provide overseas radio telegraph services.[2] As a means
of communication, radio's facilities are limited. Radio
transmission, the transfer of messages by electromagnetic radiation through space rather than along
wires or cable, makes use of the frequency spectrum,
a limited natural resource.[3] Two radio transmission
systems may not employ the same frequencies at the
same time in the same area without interfering with
one another. Thus there is a fixed natural limitation
upon the number of stations that can operate without
interfering with one another. Prior to World War I,
questions of interference arose rarely because there
were more than enough frequencies for the existing
number of stations and the state of the art.[4]

---

[2]Kurt Borchardt, Structure and Performance of
the U.S. Communications Industry (Boston: Harvard
University Press, 1970), p. 46.

[3]This is a range of frequencies (rates of oscil-
lation) of electromagnetic radiation. A radio differentiates between two or more electromagnetic signals or
frequencies just as the ear differentiates between
different frequencies of sound, such as different notes
of music or different voices.

[4]Donald M. Gillmor and Jerome A. Barron, Mass
Communication Law, second edition (St. Paul, Minnesota:
West Publishing Company, 1974), pp. 763-764.

On August 13, 1912, the Radio Act of 1912 received the approval of both the Senate and the House and became law. It provided that anyone operating a radio station must have a license issued by the Secretary of Commerce. The main difference between the Act and previous bills that had been introduced was that specific regulations were now set out in the Act whereas, previously, power to make regulations had been given to the Secretary of Commerce.[5] Although the Act was primarily designed for maritime communication and "safety at sea" was the reason usually cited for its introduction, R. H. Coase notes that public business such as wireless telegraphy was being hindered and that the true intent of the Act was to bring about government control of the operations of the industry as a whole.[6]

The war accelerated the development of radio and the broadcast industry came into being in the early 1920's. By November 1, 1922 there were 564 broadcasting stations in the United States and Mr. Herbert Hoover, as Secretary of Commerce, was respon- sible for the administration of the 1912 Act.[7] The

---

[5] R. H. Coase, "The Federal Communications Commission," The Journal of Law and Economics, 2 (October, 1959), pp. 2-3.

[6] Ibid. Each radio station considered itself in- dependent and a state of chaos existed in many places where numerous stations tried to communicate simultaneously.

[7] Ibid., p. 5.

first government/industry Radio Conferences were held
in 1923, 1924 and 1925 at which recommendations were
proposed to strengthen control over the establishment
of radio stations and frequency allocations. The
problem was that there were now more stations than
could freely operate on available frequencies and
Hoover was attempting to find room for everyone by
limiting station's power output and hours of operation.[8]
Although bills were introduced in Congress embodying
such restrictions, none were passed into law. The
Secretary attempted to carry out the intent of the
1912 Act by inserting detailed conditions into the
licenses, and declined renewals if conditions were
not complied with. However, Hoover's attempts were
seriously undermined when the United States Court
of Appeals for the District of Columbia Circuit ruled
that the Secretary of Commerce lacked legal authority
for such actions, concluding that Congress had never
intended to delegate such authority to the Secretary
of Commerce thus leaving him powerless to deal with
the situation.[9]

In July, 1926, as a stop-gap measure designed
to prevent licensees from establishing property

---

[8]Gillmor and Barron, Mass Communication Law,
p. 763.

[9]Erwin G. Krasnow and Lawrence D. Longley, The
Politics of Broadcast Regulation (New York, New York:
St. Martin's Press, Inc., 1973), p. 10.

rights in frequencies, both houses of Congress passed
a joint resolution that no license should be granted
for more than ninety days for a broadcast station or
for more than two years for any other type of station.
When Congress reconvened that December, the House and
Senate quickly agreed on a comprehensive measure for
the regulation of the radio industry. This Act, which
became law in February, 1927, brought into existence
the Federal Radio Commission.[10] At this point the
telephone and telegraph industry had not yet been
identified with the radio industry but was "regulated"
separately, to a minor extent, by other elements of
government.

a. Common Carriers Defined

Using the example of transportation, the
Encyclopedia Britannica's discussion of carriers is
subdivided into common carriers and contract carriers.
Common carriers are defined as being those who "hold
themselves out" to serve all; their charges, schedules,
and routes are regulated, they are bound to serve all
without discrimination and are entitled to a fair
return on their investment; a "certificate of convenience and necessity" is required for operation and
interstate business is subject to regulation by the

---

[10]Coase, "The Federal Communications Commission,"
p. 6.

Interstate Commerce Commission. Contract carriers differ in that they are not restricted to serving on fixed routes at regulated rates, except when the protection of the common carriers from such competition is essential to the public welfare.[11] At the time of the Radio Act and the FRC, the telephone and telegraph industries fit this definition of common carrier exactly.

The Federal regulation of business is based on Article I, section 8 of the Constitution, in which Congress is given the power "to regulate commerce. . . among the several states". Consequently, it is Congress that is primarily charged with the regulation of activities affecting interstate commerce.[12] This power has been delegated to "independent regulatory agencies" through general legislative statutes. Since communications by wire had grown up with the railroads, it had been placed under the regulatory jurisdiction of the Interstate Commerce Commission, not the FRC. However, during the period 1910 to 1934, the ICC had dealt with only eight telegraph rate cases, four

---

[11]Encyclopedia Britannica, 1973, Vol. 4, p. 965. Regulation protects the common carrier from his competitors but not necessarily from another technology.

[12]Gillmor and Barron, Mass Communication Law, p. 59. See the opinion of Mr. Chief Justice Vinson, American Communications Association CIO vs. Douds.

telephone rate cases and two cable rate cases.[13]
With so little activity, it might be rightly said
that actual government regulation of the telephone/
telegraph industry did not start until later. This
can also be considered a bit tardy since, according
to common carrier statistics, the assets of the
American Telephone and Telegraph Company (AT&T) alone
had reached more than $5 billion by 1934.[14]

b. Domestic Common Carrier History

In the early days of telephony through the
1880's, the Bell Telephone Company dominated the
industry through a strong patent position, which it
vigorously defended against all competitors. Seventeen
years after telephone communications had originated
there were 266,431 stations operating--all owned by
Bell. The expiration of the basic telephone patents
in 1893 and 1894 marked the end of the Bell System's
complete monopoly over the telephone field and numerous
independent telephone companies and manufacturers were
formed. They offered competing services and stimulated
the growth of the telephone industry. Less than

---

[13]Eston T. White, Utilities: Electricity, Gas,
Telecommunications (Washington, D.C.: Industrial
College of the Armed Forces, 1972), p. 113.

[14]Based on quoted common carrier statistics in
Stuart L. Mathison and Philip M. Walker, Computers and
Telecommunications: Issues in Public Policy (Englewood
Cliffs, New Jersey: Prentice Hall, Inc., 1970), p. 2.

fifteen years later, the independent telephone companies
owned 3.0 million stations compared to Bell's 3.1
million stations.[15]

However, in 1907, when Baker-Morgan banking
interests gained control of the Bell system, Theodore
Vail became its new president and reversed a number of
Bell policies, emphasizing absorption of the competition.[16] Now called American Telephone and Telegraph
(AT&T), the company had accumulated enough local
operations to take over the industry simply by wielding
financial and political power.[17] AT&T initially
divided the industry with Western Union, telephone for
the former and telegraph for the latter. Having thus
neutralized its strongest telephone competitor by
this action, it consolidated long distance networks
and began to absorb the independents who were unable
to compete. AT&T soon dominated the long distance
service and no regulations or genuine authority
existed at that time which required them to provide
for interconnection with independent systems that
remained.

---

[15]Richard Gable, "The Early Competitive Era in
Telephone Communication, 1893-1920," Law and Contem-
porary Problems, 34 (Durham, North Carolina: Duke
University, 1969), pp. 343-344.

[16]Ibid., p. 345.

[17]"Independent Phone Companies: The Best Kept
Growth Secret," Business Week, May, 1973, pp. 86-87.

The Bell system's acquisition attempts were strongly resisted by the independents; but only through threatened nationalization did the government, during the Wilson Administration, stop AT&T's rout of the independents. AT&T, in varying degrees, had refused to interconnect with independent exchanges for long distance service. The independents, complaining to Attorney General George Wickersham, charged Bell with antitrust violations. The complaints were resolved by the Kingsbury Commitment of 1913, which was an AT&T-offered compromise that in reality had no impact on its dominant position in the industry.[18]

2. The Federal Communications Commission

In response to a request from President Roosevelt for a study of the organization of radio regulation, in January 1934 Secretary of Commerce Daniel Roper issued a report recommending the consolidation of the communications regulatory activities of the FRC, the Interstate Commerce Commission (ICC), the Postmaster-General, and the President into "a new or single regulatory body

---

[18] Gable, "The Early Competitive Era," pp. 352-353. Under this commitment, which was an agreement between the Attorney General and AT&T Vice President N. C. Kingsbury (drafted by Kingsbury), the Bell System agreed not to acquire control over any competing company (but it did not restrict Bell from acquiring noncompeting telephone companies!) and to interconnect independents with its own system providing the former's equipment met Bell standards (between 1913-1917, Bell purchased over 241,000 stations from independents and sold 58,000 stations).

to which would be committed any further control of two-way communications and broadcasting."[19] The groundwork was thus laid for Congressional action and the Communications Act of 1934 was passed.[20]

The Federal Communications Commission is the creature Congress created by that Act to execute and enforce its provisions.[21] Originally intended to regulate the fledgling radio industry,[22] the Act also made various organizational changes to the Federal Radio Commission and gave the agency broad powers over all communications, including telephone and telegraph (Title III of the 1934 Act, which dealt with radio, was almost identical with the Radio Act of 1927).[23] The language was broad in scope and was capable of

---

[19]Krasnow and Longley, The Politics of Broadcast Regulation, p. 14. For further details see Senate Committee Print, S. Doc. 144, Study of Communications by an Interdepartmental Committee, 73rd Congress, 2nd session, 1934.

[20]The Communications Act of 1934, with Amendments and Index Thereto (Washington, D.C.: U.S. Government Printing Office).

[21]Krasnow and Longley, The Politics of Broadcast Regulation, p. 7. Also see Title I, section 1 of the Act.

[22]Bary Taub, "Federal Communications Commission Regulation of Domestic Computer Communications: A Competitive Reformation, " Buffalo Law Review, 22 (Spring, 1973), p. 951.

[23]Krasnow and Longley, The Politics of Broadcast Regulation, pp. 11-14. The Act defined a common carrier as "any person engaged as a common carrier for hire, in interstate or foreign communication by wire or radio."

application to a host of other activities.[24] The Act
also established that the Commission's powers were
not limited to the engineering and technical aspects
of regulation of radio communications but rather to
the "larger and more effective use of radio in the
public interest."[25]

Congress acted upon the knowledge that if the
potentialities of radio were not to be wasted, regulation was essential. The facilities of radio were not
large enough to accommodate all who wished to use them.
Methods were needed for choosing from among the many
who applied. Congress itself committed this task to
the Commission providing as a touchstone the "public
interest, convenience or necessity."[26]

a.   The Public Interest

As far as domestic common carrier regulation is
concerned, the "public interest" factor seems to be

---

[24]Taub, "FCC Regulation of Domestic Computer
Communications," p. 951. The applicability of the
Act to communication satellites was addressed at the
time of COMSAT and again during the DOMSAT proceedings.

[25]Gillmor and Barron, Mass Communication Law,
pp. 764-765.

[26]Coase, "The Federal Communications Commission,"
pp. 12-13. Extracted from Mr. Justice Frankfurter's
opinion in NBC v. United States, 319 US 190, 213 (1943).
The concept of "public interest" was introduced into
American legal thought by Munn v. Illinois, 94 US 113
(1876) and is further discussed in Loevinger, "Regulation and Competition as Alternatives", Chapter III,
note 154, pp. 128-135.

something recognizable but difficult to define. Former
FCC Chairman Dean Burch, in a speech before the
American Bar Association, defined the public interest
as those actions which:

> create a prevailing climate in which
> the widest possible range and variety
> of services are provided to the public
> by the greatest practical number of
> independent entities, each one seeking
> to satisfy public wants in its own way.[27]

By this definition, "public interest regulation"
appears to be less than twenty years old, even though
the regulator and his charter have existed for over
twice that long and the telephone and telegraph
industries have existed for over five times that long.
Even the brief history of the industry's development
prior to 1934 that has been presented shows that
government regulation merely gave official approval
to the historical accidents that had shaped the business
and failed to provide national guidelines. A cursory
look at the development of the industry from 1934 to
1959 lends additional support to this view. There was
in fact little demonstrated action "in the public
interest" shown by the carrier regulators prior to
1959, when the Commission's policy of increased

---

[27]Dean Burch, "Public Utility Regulation:
In Pursuit of the Public Interest," Public Utilities Fortnightly (September, 1973), p. 70. Burch
was Chairman during the key years for DOMSAT policy
formulation (October 31, 1969 to March 8, 1974).

competition was adopted.[28]

The public interest considerations in the use of communications satellites involve more than just the question of trying to develop competition in the interest of the consumers. Some believe that it is important to secure maximum utilization of satellite systems to accomplish purposes in education and health, and other fields which economically are unprofitable but which have great social implications.[29] Others see the satellite as a means to break AT&T's monopoly of the common carrier industry and as a cost-cutting alternative to existing long-distance costs. The "public interest" in satellites means many things and the diversity of congressional opinions on the subject of satellite communications, which is discussed in Chapter II, provides an excellent example of this. Since the issues surrounding DOMSAT were as complex as the common carrier industry itself, a brief description of the Nation's primary domestic communications carriers is believed to be necessary

[28]This refers specifically to the Commission's Above 890 decision, when private ownership of micro-wave communications systems was first authorized. For more details see notes 74 and 76, infra. This seems to be an agreed upon milestone; see Taub; note 22, supra, p. 963; also Trebing, note 40, infra, p. 309.

[29]Thomas P. Murphy, "Technology and Political Change: The Public Interest Impact of COMSAT," The Review of Politics, 33 (July, 1971), p. 424.

for a better understanding of the DOMSAT discussions.

b. The Regulated Common Carriers

The magnitude of today's telephone and telegraph systems is something that may not be visible to the average user. People often refer to Bell Telephone or Western Union as big and think no more of it. One contemporary viewpoint sums up competition, regulation, and the nation's telephone industry as follows:

> First of all, capitalism is the best.
> It's free enterprise, right? Barter. . .
> Communism is like one big phone company;
> government control, man. And if I get
> too rank with that phone company, where
> can I go, man? I'll end up like a schmuck
> with a Dixie cup and a thread.[30]

An uninformed public can quickly relate to such commentary and for good reason. A current magazine advertisement reads:

> The Bell System. It's an incredible
> operation. It takes a mind-bending
> multitude of cables and switches and
> gear to make all 114 million tele-
> phones talk to each other. It takes
> a master plan to keep this system
> running 24 hours a day. It takes a
> totally unified system to make it all
> work together. . . . The result of
> all this planning is, quite simply,

---

[30]Monologue by Lenny Bruce at his famous Midnight Concert, Carnegie Hall, February 4, 1961. Bruce was a comedian of the 1960's who addressed controversial situations found within our society that he felt should be spoken about, reflected upon and improved upon. While commenting on Capitalism versus Communism, Bruce found that the telephone monopoly served as a descriptive example for him and as a problem/situation in its own right worthy of his comment.

the best phone system in the world.
One Bell System. It works.[31]

The facts reveal that there are 1,785 landline telephone companies in the U.S. with operating revenues totaling more than $25 billion, with plant assets in excess of $84 billion, and approximately one million employees. Sixty-one of these carriers provide comprehensive reports to the Commission.[32] At the time of the Kingsbury Commitment, AT&T had been servicing about 5.1 million telephones while some 20,000 independent telephone companies were serving about 3.6 million telephones.[33] Today, in comparison, AT&T services approximately 109 million telephones while the 1500 independents serve the remaining 24 million telephones of the nation's system.[34] A rough breakdown of the industry is as follows:

    (1) AT&T (23 operating companies)--82 percent

    (2) GT&E (30 operating companies)--8 percent

    (3) Eleven holding companies and large

---

[31]"Bell System Advertisement," _Smithsonian_, Vol. 6, No. 7 (October, 1975), pp. 31-32. As this is a national magazine, the reader might easily misinterpret the "totally unified system" as being his or her national telephone system.

[32]U.S. Superintendent of Documents, 39th Annual Report/Fiscal Year 1973, Federal Communications Commission (Washington, D.C.: Government Printing Office, Stock No. 0400-00284), p. 287.

[33]Borchardt, _Structure and Performance of the U.S. Communications Industry_, p. 29.

[34]"Independent Phone Companies: The Best Kept Growth Secret," p. 84.

independents--6 percent

(4) 1,500 small independents--4 percent
The Bell companies serve approximately one-third of
the geographical area of the United States and the
independents serve a second third of the country.
The remaining third is too sparsely populated to
economically service by the traditional means of wire
and cable.[35]

The Western Union Telegraph Company is basically
the sole domestic telegraph carrier. Dollarwise, it is
less than two percent the size of telephone system but
because of the fact that it provides a specialized
service (in the form of record communication and
custom-built private systems), it is actually the
forerunner of the specialized carrier industry that
has been developing during the past five years and
second only to AT&T in national importance.[36] Western
Union is also the proud owner of "Westar", the first
domestic satellite system which was put into orbit on

[35]"Independent Phone Companies: The Best Kept
Growth Secret," note 17, supra, p. 85. The independents have 11,000 central exchanges while the Bell
System companies have just over 12,000. The Bell
exchanges are predominantly located in large metro-
politan centers, each serving an average of 21,800
phones. The independent exchanges serve an average
of only 1,570 phones. See Mathison and Walker, note
14, supra, p. 113 for further details.

[36]Mathison and Walker, Computers and Telecommunications, p. 6. The specialized carriers are
discussed in Chapter III since they evolved during the
time that DOMSAT policy was being formulated.

April 13, 1974.

The Bell System owns approximately 98 percent of the Nation's long-distance facilities, which inter-connect the individual telephone companies together across state lines.[37] Such business is considered interstate commerce and falls under the jurisdiction of the FCC. AT&T Long Lines, the responsible Bell operating company in this area, has not been subjected to antitrust laws because of its holdings but has instead been shielded by the protection of regulation. Long Lines actively recruited this regulatory shelter for many years and its monopoly status actually predates the onset of regulation.[38] Because of their insensitivity to distance, satellites have quickly become economically competitive in this area and have threatened to modify the industry's structure. In self defense, the established carriers have assumed a variety of positions designed to neutralize and minimize the effects of communications satellites on established markets.

Although the satellite in space represents

---

[37]Harvey Averch and Leland L. Johnson, "Behavior of the Firm Under Regulatory Constraint," American Economic Law Review, 52 (1962), p. 1060.

[38]William Melody, "Technological Determinism and Monopoly Power in Communications," Presentation before the American Economic Association, New Orleans, December 28, 1971. Other supporting historical material can be found in Gable, note 15, supra.

probably the most novel means of communications yet
devised by man, the domestic common carriers initially
looked upon this innovation as no more than a "telephone pole in the sky". However, when this technique
was implemented for international communications, the
potential impact on the domestic market became evident
and the Commission's responsibilities were increased
and expanded, as the international lawyers are fond of
saying, "ad caelam"--to heaven itself.[39]

B. The Constraints of Business and Technology

The market structure provided a setting in which
the existing common carriers, on the one hand, and the
potential entrants on the other, pursued conflicting
courses of action, subject to the constraints of highly
imperfect markets and dynamic technologies.[40] But
any policy must operate within existing technical
constraints; policy making only begins at this stage.
Revolutionary shifts in technology and aggressive
innovation may be aborted if they do not receive the
support of thoughtful public policy.

Organizational forms which would permit the

---

[39]Rosel H. Hyde, "Space Age Regulation,"
Presentation before the Midwest Association of
Railroad and Utilities Commissioners (Chicago,
Illinois: July 7, 1964), p. 3.

[40]Harry M. Trebing, "Common Carrier Regulation--
the Silent Crisis," Law and Contemporary Problems, 34
(Durham, North Carolina: Duke University, Spring, 1969),
p. 318.

greatest development of the technology and the widest
play of operating alternatives had to be considered.
This was critical since policy decisions that impact
on the market structure (and the respective roles
of competition and regulation) once made, are not
easily reversed.[41] To a large degree many of the
problems that faced the domestic industry were associated with the pressures for change that arose from
the technological advance and the economic growth of
the postwar years.

1. The Market Structure

The Bell Telephone System, the independent
or non-Bell telephone companies and Western Union
operate virtually all of the nation's common carrier
telephone and telegraph facilities. The telecommunications industry had developed under conditions of
the so-called natural monopoly. Entry of new suppliers
was restricted, if not foreclosed, with the result
that competition was almost absent as a market force.
The regulatory agency, for the most part, had confined
itself to a concern for the economic well-being of the
regulated industry and to the correction of excesses
in pricing practices.[42] But what could be considered

---

[41]Gabel, "The Early Competitive Era," p. 359.

[42]Bernard Strassburg, "New Technology and Old
Institutions," Telecommunications (June, 1974), p. 23.
Strassburg, a thirty-year veteran of the FCC, was the
Common Carrier Bureau Chief for the period 1964-1974.

a natural monopoly in some static efficiency sense
might also be considered an "unnatural" one in terms
of meeting the prerequisites for innovation and
growth.[43]

Historically, it had been assumed that communications services were provided under conditions of
natural monopoly, although the basis for this has never
been made explicit.[44] Since World War II the consolidated voice communications market had shown remarkable
stability, increasing at an average annual rate of
eight percent, the greatest imponderables were the
demands for new services such as data and video
transmission.[45]

The stakes were high for everyone involved
since the horizontal market (that is, the percentage
of all households and business firms with telephones)
was rapidly approaching saturation.[46] If the Bell

---

[43]Alfred E. Kahn, The Economics of Regulation:
Principles and Institutions, Vol. I (New York: John
Wiley and Sons, 1971), p. 12.

[44]Manley R. Irwin and Harry M. Trebing, "A
Survey of Problems Confronting the Communications
Industry in the United States," Telecommunications
for Canada: An Interface of Business and Government
(Toronto, Canada: Methuen Publishing, 1973), pp. 214-
217.

[45]Ibid., p. 216

[46]Department of Commerce statistics show that
92 percent of all homes in the United States have
telephone service today. See U.S., Superintendent
of Documents, Statistical Abstracts of the United
States, 95th Annual Edition, 1974 (Washington, D.C.:
Government Printing Office, stock no. 9324-00108, 1974).

System and the common carriers failed to establish

a strong foothold in these future markets, they

could look forward to drastically reduced rates of

growth and a significant shrinkage of their relative

importance.[47]

a. Market Economics

Economics deals with the allocation of limited

resources towards satisfaction of unlimited wants.

Resources are typically identified as land, labor and

capital plus a technology that determines their

transformation into consumer goods.[48] The technology

is viewed as a parameter like the weather, affecting

the outcome of resource allocations but itself

unaffected by them.[49]

The domestic telecommunications industry is

characterized by rapid technological advance interacting

with market changes in the level and composition of

demand.[50] However, it has also been demonstrated that

[47]Trebing, "Common Carrier Regulation," pp. 310-311.

[48]The fact that a public interest balance may not be achieved via the market system in the presence of monopoly elements provides an economic rationale for antitrust laws.

[49]Jacob Schmookler, "Technological Change and the Law of Industrial Growth," Patents and Progress; the Sources and Impact of Advancing Technology (Homewood, Illinois: Irwin Publishing, 1965).

[50]Leland L. Johnson, "Technological Advance and Market Structure in Domestic Telecommunications," American Economic Association, 60 (May, 1970), p. 204.

the quest for profit is also a primary influence on the
rate and direction of innovation, despite the large
role of other goals motivating discovery, that must be
considered. Moreover, the relationship appears bidirec-
tional, with the state of knowledge shaping and being
shaped by profit opportunities and availability of
resources.[51] It is certain that the prospect of being
permitted to enter an established multi-billion dollar
industry for the purpose of competing with the established monopoly of that industry by means of a new
technology stirred many a corporate heart.

Utility sectors commonly proceed through four
stages, as elasticities of demand vary. In stage one,
the system is invented, often leading to control by
patents. It is usually a brief period but decisive
for the form of the system. Stage two involves the
system's creation and growth; often the system is
displacing a prior "utility". Cross-subsidies are
involved and the service usually seeks regulated status
for permanence, legitimacy and market control. In
stage three, the system becomes complete as a function
of technology and market saturation and it shifts from
the offense to the defense, competing with new technologies and challenged by the users. Finally, in

---

[51]Morton I. Kamien and Nancy L. Schwartz, "Market
Structure and Innovation: A Survey," Journal of Economic
Literature, 13 (March, 1975), p. 31.

stage four, the system yields to the pressures of competition and technology and, now no longer a utility, reverts to conventional competitive procedures.[52]

William Shepherd believes that the telephone industry has been in stage three since 1947. Was it not possible that DOMSAT could be the means that would potentially break the back of the AT&T monopoly? Dr. Burton A. Kolb, a Professor of Finance at the University of Colorado, has noted that:

> A public utility usually faces severe competition only twice in its life, once when it rises to prominence and again when it is superceded by a superior technology. In contrast the industrial enterprise is subject to the continual interaction of competitive forces, including technological change. But these forces rarely are of such magnitude as the technological revolution which seriously impairs or destroys the economic value of the public utility.[53]

Domestic satellites posed such a threat to the common carrier market. Satellite technology possessed a glamour that attracted widespread public interest as well as the potential for new, better and cheaper communications services. Communications satellites threatened to change the traditional role of the

[52]William G. Shepherd, "Entry and Communications," Competition and Monopoly in the Domestic Telecommunications Industry (Lexington, Virginia: Washington and Lee University, 1974), pp. 38-39, 59.

[53]Burton A. Kolb, "The Rise and Fall of Public Utilities--An Appraisal of Risk," The Journal of Business, 37 (1964), p. 343.

domestic carriers.[54] New markets and new potential
suppliers raised the possibility of rendering obsolete
the traditional concept of "natural monopoly", a
phrase that Professor James R. Nelson of Amherst labeled
as "one of the most unfortunate. . .ever introduced
into law or economics. . .", believing that "every
monopoly is a product of public policy."[55] Looking
at the regulatory trend of the 1960's, the Commission
was definitely working toward increased competition
[the Interconnect (1968) and Specialized Carrier (1971)
decisions are discussed in Chapter III]. While there
was some apprehension that under certain conditions
the common carrier would have an incentive to operate
at a loss in competitive markets and shift financial
burden to its other services,[56] others felt that the
regulatory agency should take advantage of whatever

---

[54]Johnson, "Technological Advance and Market
Structure in Domestic Telecommunications," p. 204.

[55]Charles F. Phillips, Jr., "Domestic Telecommunications Policy: An Overview," Washington and
Lee Law Review, 29 (1972), pp. 235-236. The emergence
of satellite transmission in the 1960's has been para-
lleled by advances in land-based alternatives for
high-density routes. Discussed further in Specialized
Carriers, Chapter III.

[56]Averch and Johnson, "Behavior of the Firm Under
Regulatory Constraint," p. 1065. In a review of the
commentary on the A-J effect model, Johnson has shown
that the earlier analysis remains theoretically valid.
Also noted is that the FCC is more inclined to open the
telecommunication field to competitive forces [than in
1962] and is no longer willing to accept uncritically
the argument that a natural monopoly exists in all
cases. See L. Johnson, "The Averch-Johnson Hypothesis

competitive possibilities existed.[57] New trends in demand and technology suggested that several parts of the point-to-point [as opposed to broadcast] communications industry might be amenable to even a fully competitive structure, particularly the large-scale transmission of data and domestic satellites as an alternative to land-based transmission.[58]

b. Rate of Return Regulation

Rate of return regulation, in conjunction with the market structure, can give rise to distorted investment decisions. In establishing the level of prices charged by public utilities, regulatory agencies commonly employ a "fair rate of return" criterion, which is computed as the ratio of net revenue to the value of plant and equipment (the rate base).[59]

After Ten Years," Regulation in Further Perspective (Cambridge, Massachusetts: Ballinger Publishing Company, 1974), pp. 75-78.

[57]Donald F. Turner, "The Scope of Antitrust and Other Economic Regulatory Policies," Harvard Law Review, 82 (1969), p. 1207.

[58]William G. Shepherd, "The Competitive Margin in Communications," Technological Changes in Regulated Industries (Washington, D.C.: The Brookings Institute, 1971), pp. 86-89. It is the combination of these two parts that proves particularly interesting. It is this combined market to which the SBS filing has addressed itself (see Chapter IV). For an economic analysis of the early DOMSAT proposals using published economic models, see Stuart N. Goodman, "An Analysis of Domestic Satellite Communications in the United States," (thesis, Polytechnic Institute of Brooklyn, June 1968), 239 p.

[59]See Averch and Johnson, "Behavior of the Firm Under Regulatory Constraint," pp. 1052-1069 for an extensive discussion of the economic considerations.

Therefore what goes into making up the rate base is
very important to the carrier. His incentives as a
monopolist may be to retard the use of his inventions
in favor of more costly technology, to engage in more
inventive activity than an equivalent unregulated
carrier, or to allow excessive requirements of reliability
and quality to shape the whole direction of his technology.[60] Because regulation limits his rate of return,
he may tend to choose a more capital intensive
technology and enlarge his rate base.

The mere fact that a new entrant's rates for a
particular route or a particular service are lower
than those of the established carrier does not indicate
that the new entrant's costs are necessarily lower than
the existing carrier's long-run incremental costs for
comparable service. In order to discourage uneconomical
entry, it is essential to permit the carriers to
respond by adjusting their rates toward their own
incremental costs. Existing rates must not be frozen
to provide an umbrella protecting uneconomical competitive activity. However, at the same time the danger

---

[60]Shepherd, "The Competitive Margin in Communications," pp. 88, 96-97. High reliability to avoid
embarrassing service outages may extend the carrier's
technology far beyond the optimum. N. E. Feldman of
Rand is presently looking into what are realistic
criteria for reliability vs. requirements in communications systems. Personal interview with Mr. Nathaniel
E. Feldman, Research Engineer, The Rand Corporation,
May 4, 1976.

exists of a carrier cutting prices to the point where revenues fall even below incremental cost in particular competitive markets if it has protected revenues from other markets.[61]

Therefore, the carriers may have special incentives to "select" innovations, to invoke regulatory procedures, and to control the flow of technological information so as to minimize the probability of new entry into any of their actual or desired markets.[62] They have been seen in the past as slow to innovate and introduce new techniques and facilities.[63] In the case of AT&T, its high inertia is particularly bad in many respects. Especially during the last decade, the legal monopoly has bitterly resisted many innovations that later proved beneficial to the users in general and neutral or even beneficial to AT&T itself.[64]

---

[61]Johnson, "Technological Advance and Market Structure in Domestic Telecommunications," pp. 205-206.

[62]Shepherd, "The Competitive Margin," p. 86.

[63]Mathison and Walker, Computers and Telecommunications, p. 146.

[64]"The Five Dollar Phone and Other Fears," Modern Data (February, 1975), p. 28. Sebastian Lasher, technical consultant to FCC Commissioner Washburn and formerly with the OTP, attributes such resistance to the Maslow School of Psychology, "if the only tool you have is a hammer, you tend to treat everything as if it were a nail." See "Remarks of Sebastian A. Lasher, Office of Telecommunications Policy," International Communications Association Conference, May 10, 1974, p. 7.

Depreciation policies are another example of
the type of decisions that can contribute to an
inflated rate base. Depreciation should reflect the
economic cost of providing service and should include
an allowance for obsolescence caused by technological
advance. The depreciation policies of AT&T are based
on the straight line methodology, the use of which
does not appear to reflect the economic realities of
a dynamic industry undergoing rapid technological
change.[65] In establishing a rate base there can be
hundreds of accounting decisions that the carrier
will make that will affect his rate of return and the
cost to the customer. As former Commissioner Nicholas
Johnson noted:

> In an industry whose annual revenues
> are roughly twice the yearly income
> tax collected by all fifty states
> combined, a fraction of a percent here
> and there may amount to millions of
> dollars in phone bill savings.[66]

Convincing arguments exist which show that
conservative straight-line depreciation for ratemaking
purposes will maximize the rate base and minimize the
current charge to expenses.[67] This may result in

---

[65]Kenneth B. Stanley, "International Tele-
communications Industry: Interdependence of Market
Structure and Performance Under Regulation," Land
Economics (November, 1973), pp. 398-399.

[66]Nicholas Johnson, "Why Ma Bell Still Believes
in Santa," Saturday Review, March 11, 1972, p. 60.

[67]Irwin and Trebing, "A Survey of Problems,"
p. 228.

politically popular service rates, but it may also

constitute a major barrier to innovation and techno-

logical advance.

A 1972 Business Week article summarized these

arguments in a critique of depreciation policies:

> [I]n figuring depreciation, Bell takes
> very long equipment lifetimes. For
> example, New York Telephone writes off
> the cost of an electronic central
> office over 38 years, so it gets its
> investment back at the almost invisible
> rate of 2.6% a year. As an over-all
> average, AT&T depreciates its plant at
> a little more than 5% a year.
> From an accounting standpoint, the
> computer industry, which is also
> capital-intensive and service oriented,
> looks altogether different. Almost all
> computer makers capitalize only the
> manufacturing cost of the equipment
> they put out on rental, or about 20%
> of what they would get for it in an
> outright sale. They write off
> installation and customer service
> costs immediately as expenses.[68]

Such rapid write-offs encourage the use of new technology

and represent the opposite extreme of the common

carriers' accounting practices, which discourage

the retirement of obsolete equipment and hence dis-

courage the application of new technologies.[69]

c. Competition and Antitrust

Competing technology and the growth of new

services posed several issues which challenged the

---

[68] Business Week, March 25, 1972, pp. 57-58.

[69] Ibid.

assumptions of market structure long associated with
the communications industry. These forces confronted
the regulator with two policy alternatives. The
first policy choice was to protect existing competitors,
or more specifically to opt for a market status quo.
The second choice was to employ market structure as a
means to exploit either new technical developments,
new communications markets, or both. History and the
FCC's activities since 1959 clearly show that the
second choice was the chosen policy. Nevertheless,
concern for antitrust was always in evidence also.
This is important since fear of antitrust involvement
can act as a constraint to major companies, like IBM,
on any plans which such companies might consider in
the field of communications, leaving the planning of
new services or alternative methods for existing
services either to the existing carriers or to
companies which have fewer commitments.[70]

(1) Competition. In the telecommunications
industry, competition has been a consideration since
the early days of telegraph, when international
overseas communications services were provided by

---

[70]Borchardt, Structure and Performance of the
U.S. Communications Industry, p. 141. Borchardt
raised this thought in 1970. Perhaps the fear of
antitrust complications was a significant factor in
keeping IBM from seeking the opportunity to apply
its technological expertise to the domestic communications area until 1974.

undersea cable. In 1927 high frequency radio made
possible for the first time both overseas telegraph
and telephone service.[71] When this technology was
first applied by companies interested in its commercial
exploitation, Congress was persuaded that this new
technology should be permitted to compete effectively
with the older telegraph cable technology. Consequently
the Radio Act of 1927 prohibited mergers of carriers-by-
radio with carriers-by-cable if the purpose or effect
of such mergers was substantially to lessen competition.
This prohibition was designed to protect the development of the new technology which required less capital
from being slowed down by the older cable technology
which required larger capital investments. This was
reenacted as section 314 of the Communications Act of
1934.[72]

After the end of World War II, the demand for
new types of bulk communications services, combined
with advances in microwave radio technology, confronted
policy makers with a variety of issues challenging the
structure of the telecommunications industry.[73] In
1959 the FCC's Above 890 decision removed all

---

[71]Undersea cables for telephone did not come
until almost thirty years later.

[72]Borchardt, Structure and Performance of
the U.S. Communications Industry, pp. 46-47.

[73]Ibid., p. 25-26.

significant barriers to the installation and operation
of private microwave systems. The Commission found no
basis for concluding that the licensing of private
communications systems would adversely effect the
ability of common carriers to provide service to the
general public or that it would adversely effect the
users of such common carrier services.[74] Although
carriers could offer the communications service at a
lower rate than private firms because of the economics
of scale and the shared use of facilities, the
Commission felt that the opportunity to introduce
"competition" in the nation's system outweighed the
small social loss due to diseconomies of scale and the
nominal adverse effects upon carrier revenues.[75] The

---

[74]Phillips, "Domestic Telecommunications Policy,"
pp. 239-240. In 1956 prospective private users asked
the FCC for access to radio frequencies above 890
megahertz to develop noncommon carrier microwave service. The suppliers of microwave equipment joined in
the request. The existing policy at the time licensed
private microwave communication systems to government
and business units only when they had "special communications needs," such as a lack of common carrier
facilities.

[75]Mathison and Walker, Computers and Telecommunications, p. 117. In this case, competition is
referring to the supplying of communications equipment,
not services. The 1956 Consent Decree of AT&T had
previously eliminated two possibilities of new competition in this area. No way was provided for outside
suppliers to compete in the sale of equipment to Bell
operating companies and at the same time, Western
Electric agreed to produce only telephone equipment
for Bell system and government use. Since then it has
not bothered to enter foreign markets, regarding
itself as "fully occupied" with domestic responsibilities. See note 83, infra.

seeds of competition were planted.[76]

Competition, or more properly economic competition, implies more than just the vying for customers or markets. It also means the absence of monopoly, on either the buying or the selling side, and the absence of government intervention in the market process. It denotes a sufficient number of well informed, independent competitors so that no individual can affect the market by restricting sales or purchases. Relatively easy entry into or exit from the market must also be possible.[77] The obvious trend in FCC policy since 1959 has been towards "competition" in one way or another. But because entry into the carrier industry is determined by the Commission only,[78] the established carriers choose to call it a policy of "regulated competition," giving it negative connotations. In any event "competition" was the Commission's policy throughout the satellite issue and remains that today.

---

[76]The case was hailed as a landmark decision that "may well determine the depth of competition" in the communications industry for several decades to come. See Taub, note 22, supra, p. 963.

[77]Encyclopedia Britannica, Vol. 6 (1973), p. 234.

[78]See the FCC's 39th Annual Report/Fiscal Year 1973, note 32, p. 108. Commission approval is required before a carrier may construct, acquire or operate facilities and before it can discontinue or curtail services. Mergers, consolidations and acquisitions of property of one carrier by another must also be passed on by the Commission.

The term "competition" has aroused more emotion in connection with common carrier matters before the FCC than any other word or phrase in recent memory. Depending on one's frame of reference, it is considered either disastrous, disruptive or terrific for the communications industry. As long as the pros and cons of competition were being argued in FCC hearing rooms and Federal court rooms, none of the contentions advanced could be proven or disproven. However, since the Commission adopted policies fostering competition the action has shifted to the marketplace.[79]

(2) Antitrust. In addition to direct regulation by the Commission and its predecessors, the domestic communications industry has been the subject of antitrust action on a selective basis more than 60 years.

The first antitrust suit was threatened by the Justice Department in 1913. As noted earlier, the independent telephone companies charged that Bell refused to provide satisfactory long-distance inter-connections. In response to this pressure, Bell entered into the Kingsbury Commitment which set forth minimum concessions only.[80]

---

[79] Kenneth W. Gross, "Competition is Not a Dirty Word," Telecommunications, Vol. 10, No. 4 (April, 1976), p. 39.

[80] See note 18 supra.

In 1921, the Willis-Graham Act permitted telephone companies to merge or consolidate with competing companies subject to approval by state commissions and the ICC. This Act effectively terminated the Kingsbury Commitment and Bell again embarked on a program of acquisition. These efforts led to complaints by USITA (United States Independent Telephone Association). As a result, AT&T Vice-President E. K. Hall set forth Bell's policy on horizontal mergers in a memorandum in 1922 to the President of USITA. The Hall Memorandum stated that Bell was opposed to further acquisitions of the independents as a general policy, except in "special cases", which were broadly defined in terms of public convenience and service.[81]

AT&T is an excellent example of a holding company. It exercises control through stock ownership over some 23 operating or associated companies throughout the United States; it owns 100 percent of the stock of Western Electric, which accounts for some 85 percent of the domestic communications equipment market, and shares ownership with Western Electric of the Bell Laboratories, the research arm of the company.[82]

A major assault on the vertical relationships

---

[81]Irwin and Trebing, "A Survey of Problems," pp. 222-223.

[82]Ibid., p. 215.

of AT&T and Western Electric occurred in 1949. In
that year the Justice Department filed a suit
alleging that Western Electric had, in monopolizing
the manufacture and supply of communications equipment
and apparatus, violated Section 2 of the Sherman
Antitrust Act. The Government sought as its remedy
both the divestiture of the Bell-Western Electric
relationship and dissolution of Western Electric into
three competing firms. It was hoped that this would
introduce competition in the manufacturing and supply
of related communications equipment. The suit ended
in a 1956 consent judgment where AT&T was required
to make its patent portfolio available on a royalty-
free basis and technical information available to
outside suppliers. However, the decree, in sanctioning
the existing AT&T-Western Electric structure,
preserved the vertical relationship of telephone
carrier and telephone manufacturer.[83]

2. Satellite Technology

Artificial satellite technology, which established
one of two major technical boundaries for DOMSAT, is
less than twenty years old. The Soviet Union announced
on October 4, 1957 that it had successfully launched
the first manmade satellite into orbit around the
earth. Sputnik I, as it was called, reportedly carried

[83]Ibid., p. 223.

184 pounds of scientific instruments and circled the earth every 96.2 minutes.[84] The first step necessary for exploiting Arthur Clark's idea of communications relayed by satellite had been taken. But by 1961, it still seemed doubtful whether rocketry would achieve such accurate positioning in the near future or whether small solar-powered electronic devices could be used to establish noise-free communication links as Clark had perceived it.[85]

Clark had envisioned a system which would use three satellites, orbiting the earth in geostationary orbit, and could relay point-to-point or broadcast communications to any location on the globe. The geostationary orbit is the band of space in which satellites circle the earth at a speed equal to its rotation and appear to hang motionless above a fixed point on the Earth's surface. This band lies 22,300 miles above the equator and the number of satellites which can be accommodated along this orbit is a major determinant of potential satellite communications capacity. From its apparently stationary position

---

[84]Lloyd D. Musolf, Communications Satellites in Political Orbit (San Francisco: Chandler Publishing Co., 1968), p. 14.

[85]James Martin, Future Developments in Tele-communications (Englewood Cliffs, New Jersey: Prentice-Hall, Inc., 1971), p. 222. Orbit locations in outer space were regarded as a hostile environment for electronic circuitry. Today they seem more benign.

above the surface of the Earth, a synchronous satellite
has approximately forty percent of the surface of the
Earth constantly in view and can provide line-of-sight
communications between any two points on that surface.
The satellite has in this way introduced a new
dimension into communications technology.[86]

Frequency spectrum utilization established the
second major boundary condition. The portion of the
spectrum which is used for radio transmission is actually
very small. Although the radio spectrum is considered to
range from ten kilohertz (10,000 cycles per second) to
three terrahertz (3 million million cycles per second),
only 40 gigahertz (40,000 million cycles per second) had
been allocated through international agreement in the
1960's.[87] This is equivalent to less than 7,000 television circuits. Although frequencies as high as 300
gigahertz (GHz) are sometimes used for experimental
purposes, physical existence of the spectrum does
not mean that it is technologically or economically
useable. The higher the frequency the more sophisticated
the technology used must be. Propagation characteristics
of radio waves vary with frequency also and with

_____

[86]Roscoe L. Barrow and Daniel J. Manelli,
"Communications Technology--A Forecast of Change (Part
I)," Law and Contemporary Problems, 34 (Durham, North
Carolina: Duke University, 1969), p. 216

[87]Ibid., p. 208. A discussion of the International Telecommunication Union and the internation
frequency allocation process is found in Chapter III.

satellites in space, the attenuation and scattering of signals passing through the atmosphere and the iono- sphere must be taken into account.

a. Orbit Considerations

The orbit of a communications satellite affects the service that can be provided since it determines the amount of time a satellite will be visible to an Earth station, in what locations these Earth stations will be and how complex and expensive they must be.

Clark's geostationary approach is one option. However, even if placed at the correct height and having the right velocity, the satellite will not remain sta- tionary because of the Earth's equatorial ellipticity and perturbations resulting from movements of the Sun and the Moon. Corrections to height and velocity are required at regular intervals throughout the life of the satellite and, since it is not economic to correct the satellite too frequently, system design must allow for drift over a period of months.[88]

Random orbits, polar orbits and inclined ellip- tical orbits, using low to medium altitude satellites, are examples of nonstationary techniques. Although systems using these techniques each have applications where they provide specific advantages, such systems

---

[88]B. J. Halliwell (ed.), Advanced Communication Systems (London: Butterworth, 1974), pp. 208-209.

normally require multiple satellites for continuous coverage and expensive Earth station tracking systems. The average costs of a sophisticated Earth station today has been estimated at approximately $4.5 million. During the early considerations of satellite communication system alternatives, Bell had supported random-orbital technology although the distinctly less capital-intensive synchronous-orbit method was a possible alternative. Synchronous systems were adopted as preferred quickly after 1963 primarily because the technology necessary for deploying such systems had been perfected by an outsider, Dr. Harold Rosen of Hughes Aircraft, and was being promoted for competitive reasons.[89]

The coverage of a synchronous satellite varies with its location in the geostationary orbit and the restrictions on minimum elevation angles at the Earth stations. The minimum elevation restrictions arise from signal quality factors and increased coordination problems with terrestrial systems at the lower angles. For elevation angles greater than five degrees the

---

[89]Shepherd, "The Competitive Margin in Communications," pp. 105-106. By some estimates, this occurred at least five years and hundreds of millions of dollars sooner than the carriers would otherwise have achieved it. See Lawrence Lessing, "Cinderella in the Sky," Fortune, 76 (October, 1967), pp. 198, 201. Shepherd also notes that unfortunately there are no detailed studies of these savings in the public record. See also Kahn, Vol. II, The Economics of Regulation, p. 67.

useful arc for coverage of the contiguous U.S. ranges
from about 53°W to 138°W longitude or approximately
85°. If the elevation angle restriction is increased
to 10° the useful arc is reduced to approximately 70°.[90]
The separation of satellites on 70° of geostationary
arc would be no problem if each satellite could use
different portions of the frequency spectrum. But
the problem is not one of physical space but one of
available spectrum and of frequency interference.

b. Frequency Allocations

        Originally no exclusive frequency bands were
available for satellites in the rapidly crowding
spectrum below 10 GHz, but because of the availability
of proven techniques with terrestrial equipment in the
4 and 6 GHz bands it was natural that these bands
should be initially used for satellite communications
and shared with terrestrial systems. But the clearly
dominant consideration for future spectrum utilization
is the advent of the communication satellite. In
1966, the existing technology made the satellite use
of frequencies to about 15 GHz feasible and had the
potential of extending that range by an order of

        [90]Dale Hatfield, "A General Analysis of Domestic
Satellite Orbit/Spectrum Utilization" (Washington, D.C.:
U.S. Department of Commerce, Office of Telecommunica-
tions, PB 207397, December 13, 1971), p. 9.

52

magnitude.[91]

Using the 4 and 6 GHz bands with approximately three degrees of orbital separation between satellites and ten degree minimum elevation angles, some 24 satellites could be accommodated each using the total band for up and down transmission interference. Each satellite could have up to twenty-four 40 megahertz (40 million cycles per second) channels, each capable of up to 1,200 voice circuits or one television circuit per channel. But one of the most important parameters in determining minimum orbital spacing is Earth station antenna size. Antennas for such satellite systems would have to be on the order of one hundred feet in diameter for acceptable performance. At higher frequencies, particularly those above 10 GHz interference is less likely to be a problem with terrestrial systems and trade-offs can be made betweeen the size and space parameters of a satellite system.[92]

Because of ionospheric effects and high noise levels, the low limit on frequencies for use in satellite links is around 70 megahertz (MHz). Until about 10 GHz,

---

[91]Report by the Telecommunication Science Panel of the Commerce Technical Advisory Board, "Electromagnetic Spectrum Utilization--The Silent Crisis" (Washington, D.C.: U.S. Department of Commerce, October, 1966), p. 10.

[92]For additional information on this subject, see D. M. Jansky and M. C. Jeruchim, "Technical Factors and Criteria Affecting Geostationary Orbit Utilization." Communication Satellites for the 70's (Cambridge, Massachusetts: The MIT Press, 1971).

transmission is relatively free and then additional
path loss, caused by rain, clouds, or fog, begins to
reduce efficient transmission. Higher powered
satellites and highly directive antenna systems can
be used to overcome some path loss problems. Modern
solar panel arrays can provide a satellite with up
to five kilowatts of power for operation if necessary.[93]

Hypothetical systems have emerged from studies
by Bell and others which have projected the possibilities for future satellite systems. Labeling spectrum
and orbit space as "precious and limited resources
which must be conserved", a system using frequencies in
the 20 and 30 GHz bands was "designed" that used 50
satellites and 50 Earth stations and could offer up
to 100 million voice circuits or equivalent. Each
satellite weighed about five tons, used digital
technology and had a total capacity of about four
million voice circuits. Such systems far surpass
today's needs but future telecommunications requirements may require such systems to be developed.[94]

. . . .

Except for the brief period of time around the
turn of the century there was little if any true

---

[93]A more detailed discussion is provided in
Advanced Communication Systems, pp. 199-227.

[94]Martin, Future Developments in Telecommunications, pp. 240-243.

competition among the common carriers for residential telephone and long distance service. However, technological advances have since introduced important competitive elements into the communications industry. Although regulation of the carriers appeared at first to be only an afterthought in an attempt to control the AT&T monopoly, the Commission more recently has been working hard to change its image and to take a more positive role in the regulatory process.

By adopting its competitive attitude in 1959, the FCC chose not to leave initiative for the services to the public that the new technologies could provide up to the established carriers. By authorizing private ownership of microwave systems the Commission only increased its workload and gained the disfavor of the established carriers. The industry's structure was beginning to change with technology and so was the FCC; it was attempting to serve the public interest.

The FCC was primarily established to insure that there was equity, order and efficiency in the assignment of the radio frequency spectrum. Technological advances in the use of this spectrum after World War II posed no major problem for the Commission, for Congress had given the agency, through the broad language of the 1934 Communications Act, the leeway it needed to keep step with technology.

In making the Above 890 decision, the FCC

established the fact that it recognized the assistance

that technology could furnish to them in promoting

the public interest. The Commission embarked on a

policy of increased competition on its own initiative

and challenged the long-standing natural monopoly

thesis. As economist William G. Shepherd has observed:

> If the technology of telecommunica-
> tions prescribed a natural monopoly,
> total and integrated control by one
> system under appropriate public
> constraints might be economically
> justified. Yet the technological
> margins between "necessity"
> monopoly and possible competition
> have been in a state of flux,
> particularly in the last two
> decades and the newer "operational"
> services have tended to be both
> more lucrative and more capable
> of supporting a more competitive
> market structure.[95]

Although AT&T, through the Bell Laboratories, is

undoubtedly the Nation's leading contributor of tele-

communications technology, its monopoly structure and

financial policies appear to be ideally suited to

impeding technical innovation. But market demands and

regulation have promoted innovation and have minimized

the negative effects of these factors to some degree.

The telecommunications technology that has been avail-

able has seemed to always extend far beyond projected

near-time communications requirements. The telecommuni-

cations policy makers who confronted the communication

---

[95]Shepherd, "The Competitive Margin in
Communications," p. 95.

satellite issue were faced with the same public interest considerations that any group would have had in opening a new market that was based on a new technology. But such considerations by the FCC for domestic satellites would certainly have many factors; the impact of DOMSAT on existing market structures and the established carriers would be only one of the many that the Commission would have to consider.

CHAPTER II

THE PRECEDENTS OF DOMSAT

In the development of telecommunications policy,
a relationship equally as important as that of
Commission-to-carrier is that of Commission-to-Congress.
The FCC was established by Congress both as an
independent regulatory commission and as "an arm of
the Congress" and to Congress, this relationship may
mean independence from White House domination, but not
necessarily independence from its Congressional
parent.[1]

Congress made a major amendment to the Communications Act of 1934 with the passage of the Communications Satellite Act of 1962 and expanded the FCC
responsibilities. Sputnik I had helped Congress to
recognize that the commercial utilization of space
could promote a wide range of benefits for the public.
This could be accomplished through either the economic
improvement of existing concepts or through the
processes of technical innovation. Among all the
projected commercial uses of space, communications

---

[1] Erwin G. Krasnow and Lawrence D. Longley, The
Politics of Broadcast Regulation (New York: St.
Martin's Press, Inc., 1973), p. 54.

was the one which took the strongest foothold and offered the greatest potential.[2] During the five years that elapsed between the launching of Sputnik I and the passage of this legislation which established the Communications Satellite Corporation (COMSAT), the questions of competition, ownership, operation, markets and boundaries were all addressed to some degree by a variety of parochial interests and activities.

The Corporation's creation provided policy foundations that were examined and challenged during the development of the DOMSAT policy (as discussed in Chapter III). This makes the understanding of the functions of the Commission and Congress in this area of telecommunications and the rationale for their actions important from the onset. In the 1960's, COMSAT's relationships with Congress, the FCC and the carriers were unique and added a level of complexity to the rapidly changing environment of the Commission and to its regulatory functions. Although DOMSAT compounded these complex relationships again ten years later, the foundations had been laid by the Commission and Congress in 1962 with COMSAT.

A. The Communications Satellite Act of 1962

By means of the Communications Satellite Act

---

[2]Hans K. Ziegler, "Space Communications--A Major Candidate for Commercial Utilization of Space," Advances in the Astronautical Sciences, 28 (1968), p. 91.

of 1962, Congress created the Communications Satellite
Corporation (COMSAT). This was a public corporation--
half owned by the major communications companies and
half owned by individual investors--established to
develop a commercial, international communications
system using satellites, put it into operation and
manage it in cooperation with foreign countries.
The advent of communications satellite technology, the
aspirations of individual companies in exploiting
it, and public policies had brought about important
changes in the structure of the U.S. overseas communications system. As in 1927 with the case of high
frequency radio,[3] the government was anxious to
promote the fastest possible development of the new
communications technology [as well as an improved
world leader image].[4]

1. Congressional Hearings

As would be true with any complex piece of
legislation, the process of its enactment was not
simple. Not only had difficult questions of ownership

---

[3]See Chapter I, note 72.

[4]Kurt Borchardt, Structure and Performance of
the U.S. Communications Industry (Boston: Harvard
University Press, 1970), p. 49, 53. When the Soviets
launched Sputnik I, the U.S. had suffered a serious
blow to its image as the scientific and technological
leader of the world. The challenge not only affected
the public's image of U.S. military superiority but
also the ability of the Republican administration to
conduct foreign policy.

been raised but also there had been a change in
administrations by the time the issues had reached
their full intensity. To complicate matters, there
was no agreement on an ownership policy for commercial
communications satellites either within the communications industry or the Congress.

In 1961, the Senate Subcommittee on Monopoly
held hearings into the pros and cons of existing
government policies and established organizations for
space communications; so did the House Interstate and
Foreign Commerce Committee and the House Committee on
Science and Astronautics. More than eighteen months
passed between Eisenhower's first statement of policy
and the Kennedy legislation being signed into law.
During that period, the FCC was the first to face the
issues that were raised.

a. The Ownership Question

The alternatives of ownership for commercial
communications satellites were basically (1) government
ownership, (2) carrier ownership, and (3) private,
broad-based ownership.[5] Congressional interest was
soaring. Between June 14 and August 24, five
Congressional committees held 21 days of hearings on

---

[5]Jonathan F. Galloway, The Politics and
Technology of Satellite Communications (Lexington,
Massachusetts: D.C. Heath and Company, 1972), pp.
47-48.

communications satellites despite the fact that there was no legislation pending on the subject.[6]

At the same time, the FCC initiated a formal Notice of Inquiry addressed to the question of ownership and operation of such a venture, specifically soliciting the views of industry as to what plan of participation was considered best. Twelve interested parties responded and there was some agreement for joint ownership and operation of the system.[7] The options were being filtered through the political and psychological climate of the day.

The overseas carriers argued that potential economies of scale would be effected by treating satellites as an extension of existing submarine facilities. They proposed a joint venture whereby satellite ownership would be assigned exclusively to them. The aerospace industry took an entirely different view. General Electric and Lockheed, in particular, called for the creation of a carrier's carrier and argued that the entity's ownership should

------

[6]Horace P. Moulton, "Communications Satellites-- the Proposed Communications Satellite Act of 1962," Business Lawyer, 18 (November 1962), p. 175. See Galloway, note 5, supra, p. 11, for a breakout of the Congressional Committees dealing in communications.

[7]U.S. Congress, House, Committee on Science and Astronautics, Commercial Applications of Space Communications Systems, H. Rept. No. 1279, Oct. 11, 1961, 87th Cong., 1st Session, pp. 23-24, and FCC Docket No. 14024, Notice of Inquiry, April 3, 1961. See Chapter III, note 22.

include equipment suppliers and the public at large
as well as the overseas carriers.[8]

The response of all common carriers, domestic
as well as international, generally expressed opposition to participation in ownership by noncarriers.
As AT&T put it, such arrangements would enable hardware
suppliers, who have no responsibility to the public
for quality or scope of service, to influence the
common carriers' future undertakings.[9]

AT&T Vice-President James E. Dingman testified
before the Senate that communications satellites were
really "no big breakthrough"; they would not make
undersea cables obsolete and they certainly had no
potential for domestic use. However, the carriers were
still sincere and enthusiastic in their desire to
help advance satellite communication [the Nation needs
more public spirit like that]. He stated:

> This position may be construed by some
> as stemming from the selfish interests
> of my company which is the largest of
> the carriers involved [it's the largest
> of ALL carriers!]. Let me assure you
> that it is not.
>
> Let one thing be crystal clear: AT&T has
> no desire or intention of seeking to
> control the communications satellite

---

[8]Manley R. Irwin, The Telecommunications
Industry--Integration vs. Competition (New York:
Praeger Publishing, 1971), pp. 97-98.

[9]Lloyd D. Musolf, Communications Satellites
in Political Orbit (San Francisco: Chandler Publishing
Co., 1968), p. 25.

system to its competitive advantage. . . .
Hard as it may be for some to understand,
our sole interest is in the earliest
practicable establishment of a world-
wide commercial satellite system useful
to all international communications
carriers and agencies both here and
abroad.[10]

The Justice Department neither suggested nor
endorsed any specific plan, but instead specified
four conditions necessary for joint ventures in order
that they be consistent with antitrust considerations:

1. All interested communications common
    carriers be given an opportunity to
    participate in ownership of the system.

2. All interested communications common
    carriers be given unrestricted use (on
    nondiscriminatory terms) of the facili-
    ties of the system whether or not they
    elect to participate in ownership.

3. All interested parties engaged in the
    production and sale of communications
    and related equipment be given an
    opportunity to participate in ownership
    of the system.

4. All interested parties engaged in the
    production and sale of communications
    and related equipment be given unrestrict-
    ed opportunity to furnish such equipment
    to the system whether or not they elect
    to participate in ownership.[11]

By reporting on its Notice of Inquiry, the FCC
was the first agency to confront the policy choices,

---

[10]Michael E. Kinsley, *Outer Space and Inner
Sanctums: Government, Business and Satellite Communications* (New York: John Wiley and Sons, 1976), pp.
9-10. Bracketed commentary added. Dingman's
testimony was before the Committee on Aeronautical
and Space Sciences on March 6, 1962.

[11]Irwin, *The Telecommunications Industry*, pp.
99-100.

and it must be noted that it acted with unusual dispatch. In its report of May 24, 1961, it stated:

> We fail to see why ownership or participation by the aerospace industry in the communications industry would be beneficial or necessary to the establishment of a satellite communications system to be used by the common carrier industry.[12]

With this observation the Commission rejected GE's plan to establish a satellite corporation, and placed the Justice Department and the Assistant Attorney General, Lee Loevinger, in a dilemma by failing to support a joint ownership policy. However, in apparent deference to the FCC, Justice modified its requirement for aerospace "ownership" rights, and substituted "participation" as its guideline for a satellite venture.[13]

b.   The Kennedy Administration Bill

The voice of President Eisenhower had been one of the first heard on the subject of commercial satellite communications:

> The commercial application of communication satellites, hopefully within the next several years, will bring the nations of the world closer together in peaceful relationships as a product of this Nation's program of space exploration. . . . The Nation has traditionally followed a policy of conducting international telephone,

---

[12] Ibid., p. 99.

[13] U.S. Congress, Commercial Applications of Space Communications Systems, p. 26.

telegraph and other communications
services through private enterprise
subject to government licensing and
regulation. We have achieved
communications facilities second to
none among the nations of the world.
Accordingly, the Government should
aggressively encourage private enterprise in the establishment and
operation of satellite relays for
revenue-producing purposes.[14]

But by the Fall of 1961, the Washington environment had

changed. The Kennedy Administration was now in the

White House and the COMSAT controversy was fully

monopolizing Congress.

President Kennedy viewed Eisenhower's policy as

"turning control of space communications over to AT&T"[15]

and on July 24, 1961 had announced that a policy of

private ownership and operation of the U.S. portion of

the system was favored provided that such ownership

and operation met the following policy requirements:

1.   New and expanded international communi-
     cations services be made available at
     the earliest practicable date;

2.   Make the system global in coverage so as
     to provide efficient communication service
     throughout the whole world as soon as
     technically feasible, including service
     where individual portions of the coverage
     are not profitable;

---

[14]U.S. Congress, Senate, Committee on Aeronautics and Space Sciences, Staff Report, Documents
on International Aspects of the Exploration and Use
of Outer Space, S. Doc. No. 18, May 9, 1963. From a
"Statement by President Eisenhower on the Commercial
Use of Communication Satellites," December 31, 1959.

[15]Galloway, The Politics and Technology of
Satellite Communications, p. 47.

3. Provide opportunities for foreign participation through ownership or otherwise, in the communications satellite system;

4. Nondiscriminatory use of, and equitable access to, the system by present and future communication carriers;

5. Effective competition, such as competitive bidding, in the acquisition of equipment used in the system;

6. Structure of ownership or control which will assure maximum possible competition;

7. Full compliance with antitrust legislation and with the regulatory controls of the Government;

8. Development of an economic system, the benefits of which will be reflected in oversea communication rates.[16]

The Executive Secretary of the National Aeronautics and Space Council, Mr. E. C. Welsh, was tasked to prepare a coordinated draft proposal for translating Kennedy's policy into effective legislation. By January 1962, after many meetings of the Council, constructive language evolved. The Administration's bill (H.R. 10115 or S. 2814) provided for the establishment, ownership, operation and regulation of a commercial communications satellite system and authorized the creation of a "privately owned and profit-operated Corporation [COMSAT]." COMSAT was to be financed from the sale of securities to the public which included, but was not limited to, common carriers or otherwise chosen companies or

_____

[16]U.S. Congress, Commercial Applications of Space Communications Systems, pp. 25-27.

individuals. It would not be an agency or establishment of the U.S. Government but it would be subject to the pertinent provisions of the Communications Act of 1934, as amended, and of the District of Columbia Business Corporation Act.[17]

2. H.R. 11040 Becomes Law

Opinion in Congress was now oscillating between the two extremes of government and carrier ownership and private ownership was seen by some as a violation of antitrust laws and a giant giveaway of government investments in communications satellite technology.[18] In an August 1961 letter to the President, the liberal Democrats in Congress (three Senators and thirty-two Representatives) had urged that a hasty decision on the space communications issue not be made in order that the general "national interest" might be determined. However, there was still no agreement within Congress as to what the national interest was nor how it could best be determined or served.

---

[17]Musolf, Communications Satellites in Political Orbit, pp. 57-58.

[18]Galloway, The Politics and Technology of Satellite Communications, p. 52. Senator Kefauver, Chairman of the Subcommittee on Antitrust and Monopoly, led the opposition. Assistant Attorney General Loevinger noted that the technology was made possible through government-sponsored R&D mainly because there was national interest in the establishment of a satellite communications system.

a. Opposing Views

No fewer than ten bills on the subject were bouncing around Congress in 1962. In a simplified picture, the cast of characters looked like this. There was Senator Kerr of Oklahoma who favored private ownership with minimal government regulation, Senator Kefauver of Tennessee, who favored government owner- ship, at least initially, and Senator Pastore of Rhode Island, who wanted private ownership with strong government control specified in the enabling legisla- tion. The President's proposal had been introduced to both houses on February 7, and questions concerning the role of the Executive and the bill's domestic and foreign policy implications were also causing debate.[19]

The first committee report on S. 2814, the President's legislation, was issued on April 2 by the Senate Space Committee. In the House on the same day, Congressman Oren Harris introduced H.R. 11040 which was identical to S. 2814 as amended by the Senate Space Committee. With minor refinements, H.R. 11040 was passed in the House on May 3 by a vote of 354 to 9. It was then sent to the Senate, where it was referred to the Commerce Committee.[20] Senate

---

[19]Ibid., pp. 52-53.

[20]Ibid., pp. 64-65. See also note 29, infra.

activity continued independently on S. 2814. Changes
were made by the Committee on Commerce which would
restrain the monopoly and protect the taxpayers to a
far greater extent than what had been previously
proposed.[21] Senator Pastore was especially concerned
that domination by one communications common carrier
(AT&T) should be avoided.[22] The committee amended
subsection 102(c) to express the intent of Congress
regarding Federal antitrust laws and 102(d) so that
nothing in the act could preclude the use of such
[COMSAT] systems for domestic communications services
where consistent with the provisions of the act.[23]

---

[21]Musolf, Communications Satellites in
Political Orbit, p. 54.

[22]Galloway, The Politics and Technology of
Satellite Communications, p. 57.

[23]U.S. Congress, Senate, Committee on Commerce,
Communications Satellite Act of 1962, S. Rept. No. 1584,
June 11, 1962, 87th Congress, 2nd Session, pp. 13-14,
emphasis added. Section 102(c) was modified to dispel
fears that the legislation might be construed as a
total exemption of the corporation and participants
from antitrust laws. However, this action could also
be considered as an affirmation of the proposition
that competition, however qualified, is presumptively
the national policy, and that any exemption found in
the act should be narrowly construed. See also Legislative Note, "The Communications Satellite Act of 1962",
Chapter III, note 44, p. 397. The clarification of
subsection (d) was made to avoid any possible inference
that may be drawn from the other provisions of the bill
that Congress had made a policy determination that use
of the system be limited to international communications. However, the committee felt that it was unlikely
that the system would not be useable for domestic services (because of technical and economic limitations)
but that they were entirely consistent with the Act.

Debate in the Senate was turned into a strategy of filibuster by the bill's opponents.[24] As a consequence, cloture was imposed on August 14 (the first time it had been successfully used since 1927) to end debate and on August 17, the bill, which was in essence H.R. 11040 with everything after the enacting clause eliminated and the body of S. 2814 (as amended by the Commerce Committee) inserted in lieu thereof, finally passed the Senate and was sent to the House.[25] The bill won final House approval on August 27, 1962.

b. The Final Act

When President Kennedy signed the Communications Satellite Act of 1962 on August 31, one of the most controversial pieces of legislation of the 87th Congress became law and the opponents of COMSAT were finally defeated.[26]

The purpose of the Act is best summarized by

---

[24]Primary opposition were the supporters of a government-owned approach; Kefauver (D., Tenn.), Morse (D., Ore.), Yarborough (D., Tex.), Gore (D., Tenn.), Long (D., La.), Burdick (D., N.D.), and Neuberger (D., Ore.).

[25]Musolf, Communications Satellites in Political Orbit, pp. 57, 97-108. The bill that had left the House over three months earlier was hardly the same bill that was just returned. However, it was recognized that any amendments to the Senate version could be subjected to filibuster again.

[26]Galloway, The Politics and Technology of Satellite Communications, p. 69.

Sections 102(a) and (b) of the Act:

> (a) The Congress hereby declares
> that it is the policy of the United
> States to establish, in conjunction
> and in cooperation with other countries,
> as expeditiously as practicable a
> commercial communications satellite
> system, as part of an improved global
> communications network, which will be
> responsive to public needs and
> national objectives, which will serve
> the communication needs of the United
> States and other countries, and which
> will contribute to world peace and
> understanding.
>
> (b) The new and expanded telecommuni-
> cations services are to be made available
> as promptly as possible and are to be
> extended to provide global coverage at
> the earliest practicable date. In
> effectuating this program, care and
> attention will be directed toward pro-
> viding such services to economically
> less developed countries and areas as
> well as those more highly developed,
> toward efficient and economical use
> of the electromagnetic frequency spectrum,
> and toward the reflection of the benefits
> of this new technology in both quality
> of services and charges for such
> services.[27]

With respect to the Communications Act of

1934, the COMSAT Act states that the corporation

that was created by the Act [Communications Satellite

Corporation] shall be fully subject to the provisions

of the Communications Act. However it further

states that:

> Whenever the application of the
> provisions of this Act shall be

---

[27]The Communications Satellite Act of 1962,
Pub. L. No. 87-624, 87th Congress, 2nd Session
(August 31, 1962), 76 Stat. 419. Emphasis added.

> inconsistent with the application
> of the provisions of the
> Communications Act, the provisions
> of this Act shall apply.[28]

In creating COMSAT as a joint venture, subject to Government influence but owned and operated by broad-based private interests, Congress rejected a number of alternatives such as completely governmental projects (like the Atomic Energy Commission or the Tennessee Valley Authority), purely commercial joint ventures, and single-company operations.[29]   COMSAT, like the FCC, is a creature of Congress, but not by accident. It was not created because "no entry would otherwise take place." The Government or AT&T could have acted alone or separate companies could have established individual segments of a global relay.[30]

Rapid development was a strong consideration (Kennedy's criteria--"at the earliest practicable date"--was in partial response to a projected deficiency in international communications capability

---

[28]Ibid., Section 401.

[29]Harvey J. Levin, "Organization and Control of Communications Satellites," University of Pennsylvania Law Review, 113 (January, 1965), p. 324.

[30]AT&T was obviously in the best position to develop the system. Success with Telstar (a wholly Bell-sponsored random-orbit communications satellite which was launched in July 1962) indicated both capacity and desire for vigorous independent action. To this could be added the company's great financial resources, which might have been considerably augmented by such foreign participants as the British Post Office.

and to meet the alleged requirements of national prestige in the "cold war"), probably stronger than commercial considerations would have dictated. If time had been of no concern, the country might have waited until the market could support multiple independent private systems or joint ventures limited to parties without vested communications interests.[31] On the basis of costs, single-company ownership would have been easily possible, especially if NASA had charged no more than marginal costs for launching and tracking. Despite these considerations, opposition to a single-company ownership was overwhelming in view of the threat of monopoly, accompanied by anti-trust and regulatory problems. Single-company ownership, in fact, was never *formally* proposed in Congress.[32]

The remedy which Congress finally selected was thus obviously not Commission regulation pure and simple. It was instead a set of special techniques intended to produce, by internal organizational constraints, some of the results that a competitive economic structure would have produced externally.[33]

---

[31]Levin, "Organization and Control of Communications Satellites," pp. 325, 356.

[32]Ibid., pp. 332-333.

[33]Ibid., p. 338.

B. Space Age Regulation

The burden of satellite communications regulation falls primarily on the FCC. The COMSAT legislation imposed elaborate direct controls by the Commission on this "common carrier's common carrier", more comprehensive and more complex than any of the regulatory apparatus that had been used previously for the supervision of traditional communications carriers. In its expanded role, the Commission could require additional facilities from COMSAT if called for by the public interest. It could authorize construction, operation and ownership of ground terminal stations of the system by the Corporation, or by private communications carriers, or the two jointly. In general, the FCC was empowered to "make rules and regulations to carry out the provisions of this Act."[34]

The Commission now had an additional opportunity to expand on its competitive communications policy. It was evident to the drafters of the legislation that the new COMSAT Corporation would have to consider the many public and national interest considerations inherent in this new area of endeavor. Consequently to insure that all interests were faithfully considered, Congress had applied a scheme of regulation that was literally

[34] "Communications Satellite Act of 1962," Harvard Law Review, 76 (1962), pp. 390-391. See also Levin, "Organization and Control of Communications Satellites," p. 316.

unprecedented.[35] An example of the Commission's

added duties in satellite matters is typified by the

following excerpt from the Act which required the

Commission to:

> insure effective competition,
> including the use of competitive
> bidding, where appropriate, in
> the procurement by the Corporation
> and communications common carriers
> of apparatus, equipment, and
> services for the establishment
> and operation of the communications
> satellite system and satellite
> terminal stations.[36]

In the exercise of its new authority, the

Commission was quickly confronted with essentially

three new considerations which surfaced. The use of

outer space for communications had international

ramifications that required some rethinking of the

traditional international frequency allocation

process that had developed through the efforts of

the International Telecommunications Union (ITU) and

its predecessors since 1903. In addition, this new

technology offered cost and performance advantages

that were attractive to both the carriers and businesses

---

[35]Rosel H. Hyde, "Space Age Regulation," Presentation before the Midwest Association of Railroad and Utility Commissioners (Chicago, Illinois: July 7, 1964), p. 5. The COMSAT Act includes provisions where the Commission could actually direct COMSAT to establish communications to a particular part of the world, regardless of whether it was profitable or not, if the Secretary of State advised that it was in the national interest.

[36]The Communications Satellite Act of 1962, Pub. L. No. 87-624.

alike and questions of who was authorized to use the
COMSAT system were quickly raised. Finally, in 1965,
these questions gave birth to the idea of applying
satellite communications technology to domestic
communications applications and the domestic satellite
policy issue was placed before the Commission.

1. International Considerations

Satellites, which are oblivious to national
borders and physical obstructions such as mountains,
oceans and great distances, make the distinction
between domestic and international communications a
purely artificial one.[37] As the era of space communications progresses, it is important to recognize its
impact on other nations of the world.[38]

Just as nations feel that a stockpile of
weaponry is imperative for security and prestige, so
too, is it believed that a domestic satellite link for
communications is a guarantee for independence and
status.[39] The power elites of the developing countries

---

[37]Kinsley, Outer Space and Inner Sanctums, p.
137.

[38]Neil P. Hurley, "Satellite Communications,"
America, 115 (August 27, 1966), p. 204.

[39]Ibid., p. 206. Although it was the express
wish of President Kennedy that the envisioned system
of satellite communications be truly global, "national"
motives represent the most difficult obstacle to this
and it's hard to see how a proliferation of satellite
systems can be avoided.

are eager for the communications power that satellites might help to provide, consolidating national power and promoting a sense of national unity and loyalty.[40] Although the considerations imposed by nationalism are becoming more pertinent in today's international arenas with the emergence of each new nation, this thought is only identified here as an international consideration to be addressed by the determiners of future telecommunications policy in forums like the ITU.

The basic questions that were addressed by the FCC in its communications satellite policy decisions were those that evolved from the use of international resources for the development of this technology. These decisions were important since they represented initial policy. It is reasonable to believe that future generations of all nations are either influenced or constrained considerably by these policies or by whatever systems of satellite communications or related systems of international policy that result. The question of geostationary orbit utilization represented a unique factor for consideration in the FCC policy-making process.

a. The International Telecommunication Union

The creation of the International Telegraph

---

[40]O. W. Riegel, "Communications by Satellite: The Political Barriers," Quarterly Review of Economics and Business, 11 (1971), p. 34.

Union, the predecessor of the ITU, was the first
important step toward removing artificial barriers to
communications; it paved the way for long-distance
exchange of messages without regard to political
boundaries. Satellite communications represent a vast
improvement in this exchange of messages both within
and among nations and at the same time create new
problems of regulation and operation which were
unimagined when the ITU began.[41]

Dr. George A. Codding, Jr., a recognized
authority on the ITU, recently noted to the Fourth
Telecommunications for Government Conference:

> The ITU performs an indispensable
> task in allocating the radio
> frequency spectrum to various
> telecommunications services; it
> performs an essential task in the
> adoption of measures for the safety
> of life; it performs a necessary
> task in registering frequencies;
> and it performs a valuable task
> in bringing together telecommuni-
> cations experts to work together
> to solve common problems and, in
> general, to share their expertise.[42]

The ITU is considered by some to be no weaker internationally than are national agencies like the FCC, when

---

[41]Gordon L. Weil, Communicating by Satellite:
An International Discussion (New York: The Twentieth
Century Fund, 1969), p. 3. The ITU is the oldest
specialized agency within the United Nations. Founded
in 1865 to facilitate international communications,
its membership is more than 146 nations.

[42]George A. Codding, Jr., "The U.S. and the ITU
in a Changing World," OT Special Publication 75-6,
Department of Commerce, December 1975, p. 9.

it comes to making long-range communications policies.
There appears to be no alternative to the ITU as there
is no acceptable alternative to orderly planning for
the use of satellites throughout the world.[43]

Since the satellite's inception, those concerned
with communications have been aware that only through
international cooperation can the tremendous potential
of this technology's application to communications be
realized. Also recognized was the need for some
international organization to coordinate and regulate
the several communications satellite systems that would
become operational throughout the world; the ITU was
the logical candidate for this task.[44]

Briefly stated, the structure of the ITU
comprises a Plenipotentiary Conference composed of all
member countries and meeting approximately every seven
years to revise the International Telecommunication
Convention, an Administrative Council that directs the
ITU's affairs between Plenipotentiary Conferences,
two technical International Consultative Committees
(CCI's), one for radio (CCIR) and one for telephone
and telegraph (CCITT), a General Secretariat with an
elected Secretary General and an International Frequency

---

[43]Paul L. Laskin, Planning for a Planet, An
International Discussion on the Structure of Satel-
lite Communications (New York: The Twentieth Century
Fund, 1971), p. 24.

[44]Ibid., pp. v-vi.

Registration Board (IFRB).

The IFRB was of primary importance to U.S. satellite communications considerations. It is composed of five elected members, with its own specialized secretariat, that receives notification from countries seeking to use a particular radio frequency; the IFRB maintains a Master Register of frequencies, and if the proposed use conforms to the regulations, gives it a legitimate status by entering it on its Register. In 1934, the vice-director of the International Telecommunication Union Bureau had defined the right of priority of an administration to a frequency as moral only and not a juridicial priority.[45] However, in practice administrations have generally observed and acted upon the ITU's notification procedure of the IFRB.

It had not be necessary to raise the problem of allocation of frequencies for space services prior to the 1959 ITU Conference.[46] It was then that the United States first proposed the assignment of ten frequency bands to accommodate the function aspects of space communications. Only interim allocations

---

[45]George A. Codding, Jr., The International Telecommunication Union (Leiden: E. J. Brill, 1952), p. 190.

[46]The space technology itself did not exist prior to 1956. See Werner, "A Lawyer Looks at Our Communications Policy," Chapter III, note 99.

were made at that time for research purposes, but the
general matter was later quite adequately resolved by
permanent allocations at the 1963 Extraordinary
Administrative Radio Conference in Geneva.[47]

By accepting the responsibility for negotiating
frequency allocations for space and earth-space
services, the ITU extended the scope of its law-making
treaties from airspace to outer space. The development
of communication satellites was instrumental in creating
new dimensions to the already complex international
legal and technical problems. The 1963 Conference
assigned to the IFRB the responsibility of the notification and recording of frequency assignments to
space satellite stations and to the Earth stations
with which they are in communication.[48]

Spectrum management is not a static affair
relating to tangible objects to which legal rights and
obligations can be attached. It is dynamic by nature
and calls for flexible administrative measures to
achieve coordination and to avoid harmful interference.[49] Since there are variations in radio wave

---

[47]Galloway, The Politics and Technology of
Satellite Communications, pp. 18, 19, 78.

[48]Erin Bain Jones, Earth Satellite Telecommunications Systems and International Law (Austin, Texas:
The Encino Press, 1970), pp. 96-97.

[49]Charles H. Alexandrowicz, The Law of Global
Communications (New York: Columbia University Press,
1971), p. 33.

length propagation characteristics, only waves of certain lengths can pass through the atmosphere and ionosphere. For this reason only selected frequencies within the radio spectrum can be used for space communications. Early frequency assignments required the sharing of channels with terrestrial services.

However, the 1971 World Administrative Radio Conference on Space Telecommunications (WARC-ST) made new options possible.[50] An eight-fold expansion in the radio spectrum for point-to-point satellite communications, suitable for use during the 1970's was allocated by the 1971 WARC-ST to be effective January 1, 1973. This announcement [in August 1971] certainly was an important factor in the final DOMSAT decision. For the first time millimeter-wave frequencies (above 30 gigahertz) were available and frequency allocations were made for satellites in the bands above 10 GHz.[51] Although in the higher bands, signals are heavily absorbed due to clouds, rainfall and the atmosphere itself, the bandwidths available are much higher which permits satellites of very high channel capacity to be constructed.[52]

---

[50] Jones, Earth Satellite Telecommunications Systems and International Law, p. 97.

[51] Allocations prior to 1963 were in the 4-6 gigahertz range only.

[52] Philip J. Klass, "Satellite Radio Spectrum Expanded," Aviation Week and Space Technology, 95

The 1971 WARC-ST specifically allocated [at the urging of the U.S.] frequencies in the 11.7-12.2 gigahertz range for domestic-regional satellites in the Western Hemisphere.[53] But allocations by region [although workable for terrestrial systems] become outmoded in the face of the extensive coverage of satellites--far beyond the confines of any one region. Rapid technological change as well as the considerable increase in the number of sovereign nations involved in international communications and the ITU have added complications to the international frequency allocation process which could not have been foreseen when the ITU's structure was first established.[54]

b. Orbital Parking Slots

Concern has been expressed at many levels over

(August 2, 1971), p. 14. Much of the required technology needed to use these frequencies was then available or soon to be. Four of the eight original proposals submitted for DOMSAT systems included these frequencies as well as the then existing 4-6 gigahertz band. The allocation was slightly higher than had been proposed by the U.S. but was expected to be superior because of reduced interference problems with existing terrestrial services. This consequently required slight modification to those DOMSAT proposals. The SBS proposal, which would not be filed until December 22, 1975, would also plan to use the higher frequencies.

[53]"U.S. Gets Space It Wanted," Broadcasting, 81 (July 26, 1971), p. 44. This is Region 2. For a detailed discussion of the 1971 WARC-ST allocations, see "The World Administrative Radio Conference for Space Telecommunications, Geneva, 7 June-17 July 1971," Telecommunications Journal, 38 (October, 1971), pp. 673-682.

[54]Weil, Communicating by Satellite, pp. 6, 8.

the sufficiency of the supply of orbital slots over the
equator to accommodate the present and future requirements for communications satellites in the American
hemisphere. The limits of the spectrum are known, thus
making it a finite resource that must be allocated
carefully. While space in comparison may seem limit-
less, the development of the geostationary satellite
has quantified it to some degree.[55] For example,
the service arc for U.S. continental coverage is
approximately 70° wide (based on elevation angles of
greater than 10°). With 3° of orbital spacing to
minimize frequency interference, the 24 orbit locations
could be filled with a total space segment investment
of less than a billion dollars.[56]

Orbital slots have been analogized to land on a
frontier, waiting to be preempted by the first comer;
but squatters rights are not the answer as a look at
the frequency allocation process helps to explain.
It is not possible to establish legal ownership of a
frequency assignment for a nation, a corporation, or
an individual. Under international law expressed
through the ITU for more than half a century, the

[55]Ibid., pp. 8-10.

[56]Emeric Podraczky, "Utilization of the Geostationary Satellite Orbit," Telecommunications (January,
1975), p. 30. This cost is trivial in comparison to the
huge investment that presently exists in terrestrial
systems.

radio spectrum is a world resource. It must be said, however, that the rule in frequency allocation has tended to work out as "first come; first served." Nevertheless, the ITU has never sanctioned the principle as a matter of law.[57]

The logic of radio frequency allocation involves:

1. The allocation of a portion of the spectrum and determination of minimum engineering standards for the desired service;

2. Determination of engineering standards for specific systems;

3. Determination of the allocation of frequency assignments with respect to the geographic space to be served by the signals; and

4. Determination of which organization should conduct the radio service at each of the specific "frequency assignments" produced in Step 3 (this is often referred to as the licensing of the operator).

The four steps in the process are all interrelated logically, technically, administratively and politically. The "parking slot" problem involves Steps 2, 3 and 4. More naive formulations seem to assume that Step 4 is readily available for the first comer. In reality it is much more complex and all steps are necessary. It is illusion to fancy that private property "slots"

---

[57]Dallas W. Smythe, "The 'Orbital Parking Slot' Syndrome and Radio Frequency Management," Quarterly Review of Economics and Business, 12 (1972), p. 7. See also G. A. Codding, Jr., Broadcasting Without Barriers (Paris: UNESCO, 1959).

(like homesteads) can be "staked out" on the orbital arc without some form of bargaining between interest groups being involved.[58]

In the United Nations, the Declaration of Legal Principles immunizes outer space and the celestial bodies against appropriation by claim of sovereignty, by means of use or occupation, or by any other means. In the exploration and use of outer space, states will be guided by the principle of cooperation. Articles I and II of the Declaration make it quite clear that national sovereignty is not extended from airspace to outer space. Consequently, the parking space concept is not consistent with the provisions of the Declaration.[59]

Source: Adapted from Podraczky, "Utilization of the Geostationary Satellite Orbit.

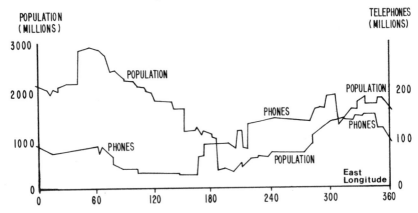

Figure 1. Population and Number of Telephones Seen From the Geostationary Satellite Orbit.

[58]Ibid., pp. 8-9, 13.

[59]Alexandrowicz, The Law of Global Communications, pp. 35-36.

Figure 1 gives a plot of the population as seen from the geostationary orbit. From this it is evident that every point on the orbit is of interest to a large number of people (300 million minimum). Also plotted is the number of telephone sets seen, which is considered to be a good indication of the voice traffic demand for satellite, although not necessarily the only one. When the geostationary orbit is viewed from this perspective, the distinction between domestic, regional or international service becomes somewhat arbitrary once again. For future systems it may be necessary to drop such distinctions for as satellites become more complex, their designs become more intimately related to the orbital positions to be used.[60]

The idea of efficiency in orbit utilization can be plagued with problems of interpretation. For example, a disaster and emergency warning system using small portable antennas may be inefficient in its use of the geostationary orbit and the spectrum but socially beneficial. Perhaps a video distribution system should not be compared to a heavy-route telephone trunk line for similar reasons.[61] Complicating the problem is the fact that there is no easy definition for "efficient

---

[60]Podraczky, "Utilization of the Geostationary Satellite Orbit," p. 31. A satellite looks at approximately 140° of arc on the earth's surface at the equator.

[61]Ibid., p. 30

orbit use" available. Not restricted to communication satellites only, the geostationary arc can also be used for other satellite systems which can provide services other than communications, such as weather tracking, resource mapping, navigation, and broadcasting. Trade-offs between the options have to be made.

2. Authorized Users

The Communications Satellite Act of 1962 made it quite clear that the Communications Satellite Corporation could not favor one carrier over another. For that very reason the Commission was required to:

> insure that all present and future authorized carriers shall have nondiscriminatory use of and equitable access to the communications satellite system and satellite terminal stations.[62]

When the FCC addressed the authorized user question, twenty-seven different interest groups filed comments.[63] The international carriers insisted that the intent of the 1962 Act had been to protect their investments by giving them exclusive rights to buy and resell COMSAT circuits. For example, International Telephone and Telegraph (ITT) argued that the carriers provided the service of transforming a "raw" satellite channel into a "useable circuit."

---

[62]Hyde, "Space Age Regulation," p. 6.

[63]This was in response to Docket No. 16058, In the Matter of Authorized Entities and Authorized Users under the Communications Satellite Act of 1962, 4 FCC 2d 421.

But users such as International Business Machines (IBM) replied that they would rather purchase raw channels directly from COMSAT.[64]

The Commission's decision ruled that COMSAT could furnish satellite services and channels only to other international common carriers except in "unique or exceptional circumstances."[65] While it declined to permit COMSAT to compete freely and directly with the carriers, it did order the carriers to reflect the large cost savings [made possible by the satellite] directly in their international rates. What was disappointingly lacking in the FCC's decision from a market perspective was any explicit recognition by the Commission that similar economic advantages could possibly have been obtained with a less restrictive ruling on COMSAT and that such a ruling, at the same time, could have freed COMSAT for effective competition with the carriers. The Commission was justified though in trying to see to it that the benefits of satellite technology were passed on equally to all customers of the common carriers, either large or small.[66]

---

[64]Kinsley, Outer Space and Inner Sanctums, pp. 50-51.

[65]4 FCC 2d 12, Public Notice 66-563.

[66]Alfred E. Kahn, The Economics of Regulation: Principles and Institutions, Vol. II (New York: John Wiley and Sons, 1971), pp. 227-233.

The Government was also required by the Commission ruling to go through the carriers for satellite service unless "national interest" dictated otherwise. The FCC was called upon by the carriers to define "national interest" more specifically when the carriers filed an appeal with the Commission over a contract that the Department of Defense (DOD) had awarded to COMSAT for circuits to the Far East. The FCC ruled in the carriers' favor and adopted a restrictive interpretation of COMSAT's authority.[67]

Two other decisions of note occurred in this period. The FCC ruled that satellite ground stations should be owned half by COMSAT and half by the carriers, reversing an earlier tentative decision of sole COMSAT ownership. Carrier interests were being well looked after but so were the interests of COMSAT.

When AT&T requested permission to build a new transoceanic cable between the U.S. and Spain, the Commission informed them that agreement would have to be established on the "proportionate fill" of both cable and satellite facilities in such a manner that both facilities reached 100 percent circuit utilization at approximately the same time.[68] This protection

---

[67]Thomas P. Murphy, "Technology and Political Change: The Public Interest Impact of COMSAT," The Review of Politics, 33 (July, 1971), p. 411.

[68]Ibid., p. 413.

of technology has striking similarities to the 1927 cable/radio competition[69] with good reason; innovation can not only have a major effect on the market structure but it can also have a significant effect on the carrier's rate base, undersea cable still being the more capital intensive technology.

3. The DOMSAT Question

The idea of using communication satellites for domestic applications was first pondered in 1964. The Hughes Aircraft Company was interested in developing markets for its satellites and as a consequence, Dr. Harold Rosen sold the American Broadcasting Company the concept of having a separate company satellite, a "national network in the sky", which would simultaneously bypass AT&T's expensive long-distance circuitry and COMSAT's unchallenged monopoly of sky-circuitry.[70] Potential Hughes' customers up until this point had

---

[69]See Chapter I, notes 2, 71 and 72.

[70]Herbert I. Schiller, "Communications Satellites: A New Institutional Setting," Bulletin of the Atomic Scientists (April, 1967), p. 7. The system would deliver network television programs. With ABC, "it is primarily a matter of economics" (i.e., comparable or better quality service at reduced rates. ABC is currently using Western Union's "Westar" for occasional service with substantial savings, as compared to AT&T terrestrial links. Letter from Mr. Anthony Cusumano, Director of Traffic, ABC, to Robert S. Magnant, May 21, 1976. Kinsley suggests that ABC's filing was partly a battle maneuver in the struggle to prevent the telephone company from raising its rates. See note 10, supra, p. 138.

been limited to the U.S. Government and COMSAT.[71]

In an application to the Commission dated September 21, 1965, ABC requested authorization for a satellite for television broadcast distribution. This made use of an inherent characteristic of communications satellites that has no exact terrestrial equivalent: the ability to deliver the same wideband message to many distant locations simultaneously. By "broadcasting" every message it receives over a wide geographic area, the satellite would provide multipoint distribution services via a single relay point.[72] An opposition to the application was filed by COMSAT and the request was returned to ABC by the FCC without prejudice pending the resolution of certain basic issues of public policy.[73] In its letter to ABC, the Commission stated:

> Your application proposed a use of space techniques which is outside the purview of the established rules of the Commission. Furthermore, the

---

[71]Charles E. Silberman, "The Little Bird That Casts a Big Shadow," Fortune, 75 (February, 1967), p. 111.

[72]Final Report, President's Task Force on Communications Policy, December 7, 1968 (Washington, D.C.: U.S. Government Printing Office, 1969), 0-351-636, Chapter 5, p. 4. The ALOHA Network also makes use of this feature. A second unique characteristic, dynamic reallocation of capacity, is to be utilized in the proposed SBS system (see Chapter IV).

[73]Walter R. Hinchman, "Public Policy and the Domestic Satellite Industry" (Washington, D.C.: U.S. Government Printing Office, 1973). A paper presented before the Interstate Commerce Commission Conference-- 1972.

        unique nature of the proposal
        presents basic questions of law
        and policy which must be resolved
        before a proposal such as yours
        could be considered.[74]

Since the Commission had a statutory responsibility
to study new uses of radio and generally encourage the
larger and more effective use of radio in the public
interest, it issued a Notice of Inquiry on March 2, 1966;
Docket No. 16495--In the Matter of the ESTABLISHMENT OF
DOMESTIC NONCOMMON CARRIER COMMUNICATIONS SATELLITE
FACILITIES BY NON-GOVERNMENTAL ENTITIES.[75]

           . . . .

Congress expanded the workload and the authority
of the FCC with the Communications Satellite Act of
1962. This national policy established precedents
which had to be considered in the DOMSAT policy-making
process. This Act only altered the framework of the
Communications Act of 1934 for the accommodation of
satellites in 1962. The Commission's competitive
perspective was still possible primarily through the
flexible interpretation of its powers and functions
under the Communications Act.

The role of Congress in the area of telecommunications policy was seen as an active one over the
communications satellite issue, primarily because this

_____

        [74]2 FCC 2d 671, Letter to ABC, FCC 66-206.

        [75]2 FCC 2d 668, Docket No. 16495, FCC 66-207.

new technology had the potential of far-reaching
implications for the public interest. Congressional
activity was also significant during the DOMSAT
proceedings (as discussed in Chapter III) but then it
was in the form of FCC oversight hearings rather than
lawmaking debate. The primary argument over satellite
communications concerned the question of ownership.
Although there was much disagreement over alternatives,
attitudes seemed to generally fear monopoly structures
and favor competitive opportunities.

The ITU has played an important role in the field
of international communications for more than a century
and offers a way to prevent clashes between domestic,
regional, and global systems. The satellite complicates
this coordinating function because of its insensitivity
to natural or political boundaries and because of the
orbit usage considerations of communications satellites.
Consequently, the need for the ITU's involvement in
communications satellite activities is well recognized.

It was obvious then that some ongoing negotiating
process involving the nations of the Americas is also
a necessity in the management of the space spectrum for
DOMSAT and regional systems. The orbital arc was
definitely a new consideration in the process; but it was
not a constraint. A single satellite could provide
domestic coverage to the U.S. However, the greater the
portion of service arc available, the greater the number

of systems that could be configured for different
purposes by different interests. The point is that
radio frequency management, including orbit considerations, is a continuing process which is not amenable
to exact legislative determination.[76] Leland Johnson
of the Rand Corporation has recently noted that:

> One of the most interesting issues
> for the future will involve the
> interface between domestic and
> international service, including
> questions of expanding the number
> of international gateways, and the
> integration of domestic, regional
> and international satellite use,
> which may involve some restructuring
> of INTELSAT.[77]

Finally, the DOMSAT question was raised by the
competitive spirit of industry, not by Congress, the
Commission or the carriers. This forced the Commission
to respond to the imperatives of this new technology,
to the user demands and to the market structure with
a viable policy. The domestic carriers dwarfed the
international carriers and represented more powerful
interests with more money at stake. However, the
COMSAT proceedings had given the Commission no indication

---

[76]Smythe, "The 'Orbital Parking Slot' Syndrome
and Radio Frequency Management," pp. 9-10.

[77]Letter from Mr. Leland L. Johnson, Director,
Communications Policy Program, The Rand Corporation,
to Robert S. Magnant, May 6, 1976. See Galloway, The
Politics and Technology of Satellite Communications,
Chapter 5 for an expanded discussion of the Interna-
tional Telecommunications Satellite Consortium
(INTELSAT).

of what the domestic market's projected demands were;
the amount of additional communications and new
services that this technology could provide or that
the market would support was still unknown. If a
COMSAT-type monopoly [or COMSAT itself] was chosen as
the structure for establishing domestic satellite
services, market support would have been a less
critical factor. However, regulated monopoly was not
necessarily the ideal device for insuring a zealous,
continuous quest for improved quality and variety of
service.[78]

---

[78]Kahn, The Economics of Regulation, p. 141.

CHAPTER III

THE DEVELOPMENT OF THE DOMSAT POLICY

Policy is a definite course of action selected
from among alternatives and in light of given conditions to guide and determine present and future
decisions. However, when the process that generated
that policy is reviewed in retrospect, it is important
to look not only at the alternatives and the given
conditions that were placed before the policy maker
but also at the cross-section of sources from which
these offerings came. In the DOMSAT considerations,
market interrelationships, policital interrelationships
and technological interrelationships were extremely
important.

Since no one had a monopoly on the public
interest, the Commission had to take into account
all elements affecting the issue. Figure 2 is
representative of the factors that the Commission
repeatedly deals with. All played a part in the
formulation of DOMSAT policy. The White House
played an expanded role in this policy-making process
and technology was seen as a force of increasing
significance, promoting an even wider competitive
environment and parallel Commission policies as

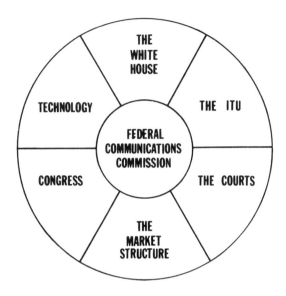

Figure 2.   The World of the FCC

precedents of DOMSAT.

A variety of policy makers and personalities
was very much in evidence throughout the DOMSAT
proceedings. Administrations changed as did Commissioners during the almost seven year period; old
voices provided comment and new voices raised new
questions. It is difficult, if not impossible, to
determine which of the forces were dominant in the
DOMSAT decision but it is essential that the existence
of all of them be recognized. However, one must bear
in mind that only one policy-making body, the
Commission, was responsible for balancing the interests
of all concerned and making the final policy decision.

A.   The Basic Issues

Not long ago the accepted standard for the economics of communications in the United States was regulated monopoly. In the changing social philosophy of the 1960's this standard held for local public telephone service but not for long-distance or private line services by ground microwave systems or satellites. The FCC decision on DOMSAT reflected this change and had an impact on the organization of a substantial part of the communications industry.[1]

The COMSAT Act left the question of who has the right to put up and operate a domestic satellite system shrouded in ambiguity. Administration and Congressional experts who drafted the Act assumed that satellites would be used mainly for international communications, at least over the next decade or so and failed to anticipate the speed with which satellite technology would develop.[2]

In the international area, the politicians had made the decision as to how communications satellite

---

[1]John McDonald, The Game of Business (Garden City, New York: Doubleday, 1975), p. 290.

[2]Charles E. Silberman, "The Little Bird that Casts a Big Shadow," Fortune, 75 (February, 1967), pp. 110-111. The assumption was that, for the immediate future, the only systems that could be operated would be low or medium altitude "random" satellites like Telstar which were basically not practical for domestic systems. However, Hughes Syncom II was operational in July 1963.

technology was to be adapted to the established
institutions. The question was whether the existing
structures of regulation and the domestic industry
could be relied upon to implement this technology
domestically or whether change was necessary to assure
public benefit. Congress used its favorite device
of saving most of the toughest problems for administrative resolution.[3] The effect of such innovation
on the existing market was one of the more complex
considerations addressed by the FCC.

Technology was compounding the issues in several
ways. Not only had the Hughes geosynchronous satellite
technology made equatorial orbital slots a desirable
commodity internationally, complicating the definition
of "domestic" systems, but now computer technology was
both assisting in performing communications functions
and increasing the demand for communications to provide
distributed computing functions. Such demands raised
new questions of competition simultaneously with
DOMSAT, promoted new policies and altered the industry's
shape a bit more.

1. A Notice of Inquiry

ABC's proposal for the construction and operation
of a satellite for a private, specialized domestic

---

[3]Bernard Strassburg, "New Technology and Old
Institutions", Telecommunications (June, 1974), p. 24.

communication requirement presented the Commission with significant questions as to the compatibility of such a proposal with the purposes, policies and objectives of the Communications Satellite Act. Believing that the public interest would best be served by obtaining the views of all interested parties before action was taken, the Commission in a Notice of Inquiry invited comments from all concerned on the following specific questions:

(a) Whether, as a matter of law, the Commission could promulgate policies and regulations, looking toward the authorization of nongovernmental entities to construct and operate communication satellite facilities for the purpose of meeting their private or specialized domestic communications requirements.

(b) Whether, as a matter of policy, it would be in the public interest to grant such authorizations and would it be technically feasible to accommodate the space services contemplated in light of existing electromagnetic interference criteria.

(c) Whether any such authorizations would impact upon the policies and goals set forth by the Communications Satellite Act and upon the obligations of the U.S. Government as a signatory in INTELSAT.

The Commission would also entertain other relevant matters to which the respondents wished to address themselves. This was the beginning. The issues of competition and ownership were being raised again and it would be almost seven years before a domestic satellite policy would be finalized.

a. The Ford Proposal

Of all the briefs, studies or statements filed with the Commission [19 parties responded on or before August 1, 1966], it was the Ford Foundation's proposal that brought the questions about a domestic satellite system to the forefront of public discussion and government decision.[4] In addition to answering the questions posed by the Notice of Inquiry, the Ford Foundation submitted a model of a private satellite system to provide for the transmission of both commercial and noncommercial television programming and called for the creation of a Broadcasters' Nonprofit Service Corporation (BNS) to establish such a system.[5]

The Ford plan was to provide a wholly new order of service--six channels for commercial networks and five noncommercial channels in each of the four time zones. This new satellite system, which had been developed by engineers, scientists and economists borrowed from Hughes Aircraft, IBM, the Rand Corporation and several universities, could provide greatly expanded

---

[4]Silberman, "The Little Bird", p. 111.

[5]FCC 2d 86 Report and Order, Appendix B at 108. This summary, which was provided with the First Report, provides excellent background on the initial responses. Appendix C discusses the legal considerations and Appendix D is the Technical Annex.

and improved transmission at much lower cost to the
commercial television networks. Similarly ABC had
estimated that it could reduce its own AT&T long-line
costs by as much as 30 percent by switching over to
satellites.[6] The system would also provide a "social
dividend" in the form of free channels to link the
Nation's now isolated educational television stations
into one or more national networks, as well as free
channels for instructional television for schools and
colleges.[7]

In Congress, the Senate Subcommittee on Communications was holding hearings on progress in space
communications and the Ford Foundation's proposed BNS
service. Senator John O. Pastore, the Subcommittee's
Chairman since 1955, had instructed his Communications
Counsel Nicholas Zapple[8] to get in touch with the
carriers, the networks, and anyone who might be
concerned with these issues "so we might have the
opinion of all. . . .[and] know from the very

---

[6]Andrew R. Horowitz and Bert Cowlan, "Should
People Fight for Satellites," Tele-VISIONS (January/
February, 1976), p. 5.

[7]Silberman, "The Little Bird", pp. 111, 223.

[8]At the time a veteran of more than twenty years
of Congressional experience, Zapple had earned a repu-
tation as a resourceful and innovative staff assistant.
His knowledge of federal communications law was considered unsurpassed on Capital Hill. As noted in
Peabody, Berry, Frasure and Goldman, To Enact a Law
(New York: Praeger Press, 1972), p. 91.

beginning what the impact of these proposals will be. . ."[9] Reporting to this subcommittee on the FCC's progress in this area to date, Commission Chairman Rosel H. Hyde noted that comments had been filed by a number of parties on August 1, 1966 and that reply comments[10] were due for filing on or before October 1, 1966. When Pastore asked him, "As you sit here this morning, do you feel that you should make any further requests of the Congress in order to expedite the development of the communications area?", Hyde replied, "No, I do not, Mr. Chairman. I believe the direction that we have from Congress will permit us to proceed expeditiously."[11] Hyde did offer, however, this perspective of the difficulties that the Commission was having in the development of policy in the communications satellite area:

> While significant determinations have
> been timely made since February 1965
> in each of these areas [the deter-
> mination of the COMSAT system's techni-
> cal description and the criteria for
> its ownership and operation], other
> problems of equal complexity and
> far-reaching effect have arisen

---

[9] U.S. Congress, Senate, Committee on Commerce, Subcommittee on Communications, Progress Report on Space Communications, Serial 89-78, August 10, 17, 18 and 23, 1966, 87th Congress, 2nd Session, p. 3.

[10] Under the Administrative Procedures Act, reply comments are routine for the presentation of opposing views and comments.

[11] U.S. Congress, Progress Report on Space Communications, pp. 17, 19-20.

[DOMSAT]. This is, of course, to be
expected in a field with a technology
as fast developing and dynamic as
communications via satellite.[12]

Pastore's boss, Senator Warren Magnuson

(Chairman of the Commerce Committee) was heard later

that year, while touring a COMSAT earth station, to

say:

I am hopeful that it [the Ford
Foundation plan] won't interfere
with the operation of COMSAT because
we made a commitment to the American
people when we passed the bill: that
if they put their investment in COMSAT
and gave it their support, then we
would do what was best government-wise
and regulation-wise to keep it going.[13]

If Congress had chosen to promote a total monopoly

posture for COMSAT over all sky-circuitry, such would

have been the determination of DOMSAT policy. Fortu-

nately this was not the case.

After reviewing the August 1 comments of all

interested parties, the Commission decided that it was

necessary and "in the public interest" to expand the

---

[12]Ibid., p. 4.

[13]Michael E. Kinsley, Outer Space and Inner
Sanctums: Government, Business and Satellite Communications (New York: John Wiley and Songs, 1976).
Kinsley devotes approximately 20 pages (pp. 138-158) to
the variety of supportive and opposing postures that
the prime contestants took in their vying for control
of DOMSAT. Although his conclusions are quick to
categorize the FCC commissioners as "inferior minds
or, at the very least, minds somewhat distracted from
the public weal," his description of the machinations
of industry gives the reader an appreciation for what
the Commission was having to deal with.

initial scope of this proceeding and to invite comment on the Ford proposal. It additionally found that the initial filings were not fully responsive to the technical questions set forth in the initial notice. Accordingly, on October 20, 1966, the Commission adopted a "Supplemental Notice of Inquiry" for additional commentary. By December 16, 1966, 21 parties, nine of which had not filed previously, responded.[14]

Four parties [ABC, Ford, COMSAT and AT&T] had submitted proposals for domestic satellite systems. Those of COMSAT and AT&T were counter-proposals to the ABC and Ford proposals aimed at retaining the former's pre-eminence in domestic and space communications activity.[15] They urged the FCC to authorize general purpose systems while the latter proposals asked for special purpose systems for the distribution of television programs, anticipating cost savings made possible by satellite technology. During the course of the proceeding both COMSAT and Ford supplemented their original proposal by suggesting pilot programs rather than full-scale operational domestic systems. The others who made their views known to the Commission included common carrier, broadcast, computer, aviation,

---

[14]22 FCC 2d 111.

[15]Herbert I. Schiller, "Communications Satellites: A New Institutional Setting," Bulletin of the Atomic Scientists (April, 1967), p. 8.

press, government and educational interests. In
addition to the ownership problem, a wide disagreement
on a broad range of legal, technical and economic
issues emerged.[16]

COMSAT's pilot proposal contemplated an investment of $58 million in the space and ground segments
to place a limited satellite system in service by 1970.
This pilot program was to last only two years (1970
and 1971) and COMSAT would own and control the system
only as a trustee or steward, with final arrangements
as to ownership and control to be postponed until the
completion of the program. AT&T expressed support for
the pilot program but asked that it, rather than COMSAT,
be permitted to own the ground stations.[17]

In 1968, Chairman Hyde summarized this early
activity as follows:

> With respect to domestic satellites,
> it is reasonable to look forward to
> the time when satellites will be

---

[16]Final Report, President's Task Force on Communications Policy, December 7, 1968, (Washington, D.C.:
U.S. Government Printing Office, 1969), 0-351-636,
Chapter 5, p. 2. A fair amount of disagreement among
owners, operators and regulators of satellite systems
still exists today. For this reason, Hughes Aircraft
(a principal builder of satellite systems for many
parties) has established a firm policy not to participate in any evaluation of regulatory actions. Letter
from Dr. Albert D. Wheelon, Vice President and Group
Executive, Hughes Aircraft Company to Robert S. Magnant,
May 4, 1976.

[17]Henry Geller, "Competition and Monopoly Policies in Domestic Satellite Communications," The Antitrust Bulletin, 13 (Fall, 1968), pp. 954-955. Geller
was FCC General Counsel at the time.

competing with, or complementing,
terrestrial microwave and cable
for long-distance telephone and
other point-to-point communications
services. The issue of how to
structure the ownership, operation
and use of a domestic satellite
system is now before us in a general
public inquiry. Its purpose is to
resolve a number of difficult legal,
technical and policy questions
involved in the use of satellites by
both carrier and noncarrier entities.
We have under consideration a pilot
program to assist in accumulating
data toward formulation of final
format for our domestic system.[18]

b. A Question of Law

In considering the question of competition or

monopoly as regards DOMSAT systems, it was first

necessary to look at the threshold legal questions,

which could have severely limited the Commission's

options with respect to ownership and control of a

domestic satellite system.[19] The primary question,

of interest to all concerned, was whether the

Communications Act of 1934 or the Communications

Satellite Act of 1962 would regulate domestic

satellite communications. Another concern raised was

whether the authorization of DOMSAT systems would

violate our international agreements of 1964 as

---

[18]Rosel H. Hyde, "The Role of Competition and
Monopoly in the Communications Industries," The
Antitrust Bulletin, 13 (Fall, 1968), p. 908.

[19]Geller, "Competition and Monopoly Policies
in Domestic Satellite Communications," p. 955.

members of INTELSAT. The various interests involved tended to interpret the applicability of these laws and agreements according to their own interests.

COMSAT naturally believed that under the 1962 Act it was the only entity authorized to have satellites, be they domestic or international, and the Ford Foundation believed that under the 1934 Act the FCC had the legal right to authorize an entity like BNS. Although some carriers asserted that the Commission had the broad powers to authorize nongovernmental entities to establish and operate DOMSAT facilities, others alleged that the legal capacity was lacking. However, all carriers agreed that such systems should not be authorized to noncommon carriers as a matter of policy. The Commission concluded that both Acts clearly empowered it to authorize DOMSAT facilities to be owned by any entity as the national public interest required and that INTELSAT agreements would not be compromised. Pertinent arguments supporting these conclusions follow.[20]

(1) The Communications Act of 1934. The broad language of this act had provided the Commission with "regulatory power over all forms of electrical

---

[20] 22 FCC 2d 128, Appendix A, Memorandum on Legal Issues. Much of the following information is more extensively developed in the Ford Foundation's legal brief; prepared in response to Docket No. 16495 by Ginsburg and Feldman, Attorneys for the Foundation, dated August 1, 1966.

communications. . . ."[21] Section 303(g) of the Act
specifically directed the Commission to "generally
encourage the larger and more effective use of radio
in the public interest." In 1961, the Commission
concluded that it had the power to authorize the private
use of communications satellites and responses from its
inquiry on the subject supported its position.[22] Prior
Judicial and Commission decisions also supported the
position that Congress had given the Commission broad
power. In NBC v. United States, for example, Justice
Frankfurter stated that "Congress endowed the Communications Commission with comprehensive powers to promote
and realize the vast potential of radio."[23]

(2) The Communications Satellite Act of 1962.
This Act did not preclude Commission authorization
of private noncommon carriers to construct and operate
DOMSAT facilities. The primary purpose of the Act was
to establish an international communications satellite
system and was intended as a major step towards a

[21]U.S. Congress, Senate, Committee on Interstate
Commerce, S. Rep. No. 781, 73rd Congress, 2nd Session,
April 17, 1934, p. 1. See also Chapter I, note 22 and
Krasnow and Longley, note 1, supra, p. 15.

[22]See Docket No. 14024, Inquiry Into the
Administrative and Regulatory Problems Relating to the
Authorization of Commercially Operable Space Communi-
cations Systems, March 29, 1961, reprinted in U.S.
Congress, House, Committee on Science and Astronautics,
Hearings on Communication Satellites, May 8, 9, 10
and July 13, 1961, 87th Congress, 1st Session, pp.
537-581.

[23]319 US 190, 217 (1943). See also Chapter I,
notes 25 and 26.

"global communications network."[24]   An international

system was seen both as a means to move ahead of the

Soviet Union (which had apparently taken the lead in

space technology) and as a way for the United States

to assert her leadership at the 1963 Extraordinary

Administrative Radio Conference of the International

Telecommunications Union (called in 1963 to allocate

frequencies for communications satellite systems).[25]

Since Telstar was seen as the COMSAT model for many

years to come, its random orbit made sense only in

the context of an international system.[26]   The language

of Section 102(d) of the Act expressly recognized the

power of the Commission to authorize private DOMSAT

systems.   Mr. Dingman, in written testimony to the

Senate on another occasion, had noted that "sometime

in the future it may be necessary to augment the

initial system and this could involve the establishment

of a new satellite system."[27]

    (3)   The 1964 International Communications-

Satellite Agreements.   These agreements did not

-----

[24]See Chapter II, note 27.

[25]U.S. Congress, House, Committee on Government
Operations, H.R. Rept. No. 178, 89th Congress, 1st
Session, March 17, 1965, p. 22.

[26]See Chapter II, notes 23 and 30.

[27]U.S. Congress, Senate, Hearings on Communications Satellite Legislation Before the Senate Committee
on Commerce, April 10-13, 16, 24 and 26, 1962, 87th
Congress, 2nd Session, p. 202.   This was in response to
questions that had been raised by Senator Yarborough.

preclude the establishment of DOMSAT facilities by noncommon carriers. The Inter-Governmental Agreement and the Special Agreement (concluded in 1964) were designed to establish "a global commercial communications satellite system." Nothing in the language of either instrument has been interpreted as precluding separate domestic systems.[28] Like the 1962 Act, they were aimed at creating a single system to serve the international needs of the more than 50 signatory nations. It was never intended to serve the membership's domestic requirements or to prohibit them from developing separate systems to meet those requirements. A possible conflict of interest could have developed if COMSAT, as the international "system manager," had undertaken a separate system.

2. Technology

The merging of the computer and communications technologies in the late 1960's only complicated the Commission's problem in developing a DOMSAT policy. As the need for computers to talk to each other increased, the wideband communications capability of the satellite became more attractive. DOMSAT would definitely increase the options available for

---

[28] U.S. Department of State, Treaties and Other International Acts Series No. 5646, International Telecommunications Satellite Consortium (INTELSAT), 1964.

the computer communications requirements.[29] As Dr.

Norman Abramson of the University of Hawaii recently

noted:

> . . .long-haul service provided
> by satellite is usually more
> cost-effective than comparable
> services provided by purely
> terrestrial links. This is
> especially true of specialized,
> higher rate services. Today
> there is little, if any,
> terrestrial capacity available
> to provide long-haul transmission
> of data at rates of one million
> bits per second and higher. To
> provide new services at these
> rates in most situations will
> require both large inflexible
> investments and new construction
> of terrestrial facilities, which
> will require long implementation
> times. Satellite systems can be
> quickly and inexpensively installed
> to establish circuit connections
> wherever the user desires and at
> the data rates that he needs.[30]

The DOMSAT issue thus had at its base a persistent

driving technology--a technology that had blurred a

once comfortable distinction between communication

and data processing.[31] Not only were the two technologies

---

[29]Letter from Dr. Robert W. Lucky, Head,
Transmission Terminal Systems, Bell Laboratories,
to Robert S. Magnant, May 22, 1976.

[30]Norman Abramson and Eugene R. Cacciamani, Jr.,
"Satellites: Not Just a Big Cable in the Sky," IEEE
Spectrum (September, 1975), p. 36. SBS plans to offer
such a service, tailored to each customers requirements, as part of its integrated (voice, image, data
of different speeds) offering.

[31]Bernard Strassburg, "Communications and
Computers: How Shall the Twain Meet?", Public Utilities
Fortnightly, 82 (September 12, 1968), p. 74.

becoming more interdependent, but they were doing it at phenomenal speed. The Commission became concerned over what the resulting impact on communications might be and initiated a Notice of Inquiry [hereafter referred to as the Computer Inquiry] to determine policy on the subject. This Inquiry was in progress throughout practically the entire DOMSAT proceeding.

To facilitate an understanding of this marriage between computers and communications, definitions for such terms as message switching systems, time-sharing and distributed networks are developed below, along with some simple descriptions of the technologies involved and some perspectives on the implications of "computercations" and the Computer Inquiry on the Commission and DOMSAT.

a. Technology Dynamics

Abramson sees the force of technology and technological change on the communications industry as probably one of the most significant factors that has influenced the DOMSAT policy.[32] Because of the extraordinary advances in satellite technology and because the Federal government itself became involved in competitive enterprise through the creation of COMSAT, no more cogent example of the force of the

---

[32]Letter from Dr. Norman Abramson, Director, the ALOHA System to Robert S. Magnant, May 4, 1976.

technological change upon economic systems can be found than the study of the evolution of Federal policies with respect to the burgeoning telecommunications industry and DOMSAT in particular.[33]

It should be noted that the technology that spawned the common carrier communications industry was one of analog transmission, frequency division multiplexing, and electro-mechanical switching. With the emergence of computer time-sharing technology in the mid-1960's, digital transmission, the continuing increase in computer applications, and new requirements for "machine communications", the idea of creating new and different transmission systems to meet these requirements was quite logical. This was evident even to the established carriers. As the Bell Telephone people put it, in a 1957 technical paper on data transmission services:

> The telephone network was developed for speech transmission and its characteristics were designed to fulfill that objective. Hence, it is that the use of it for a distinctly different purpose such as data transmission may impose compromises both in the medium and in the special service contemplated.[34]

---

[33]Thomas P. Murphy, "Federal Regulatory Policy and Communications Satellites: Investing the Social Dividend," The American Journal of Economics and Sociology, 31 (October, 1972), p. 338.

[34]John D. Dingell, "The Role of Spectrum Allocation in Monopoly or Competition in Communications," Antitrust Bulletin, 13 (1968), p. 941.

Obviously, there would be requirements for systems for data communication services where the medium was not a limitation and compromises would not be imposed.

Within a period of only two decades, the electronic computer advanced from an esoteric tool of the scientist to a pervasive participant in the processes of government, business, and education. In this short time, the computer matured from a laboratory curiosity to the world's fastest growing industry.[35] As late as 1959, however, electronic data processing was generally limited to in-house or intrafirm/plant concepts.[36]

The computer itself is a giant communications system with complex switching techniques. As the power and utilization of computers increased, it was only natural to connect the internal communications circuits of the computer to existing external communications circuits and thus provide wide geographic dispersion to the capabilities of a computer.[37]

From the communications industry perspective,

---

[35]Barry Taub, "Federal Communications Commission Regulation of Domestic Computer Communications: A Competitive Reform," Buffalo Law Review, 22 (Spring, 1973), p. 947.

[36]Strassburg, "Communications and Computers: How Shall the Twain Meet?", p. 69.

[37]Ervin K. Dorff, "Computers and Communications: Complementing Technologies," Computers and Automation (May, 1969), p. 22.

the sheer growth in message volume increased the
number of switching networks needed and the complexity
of the sophisticated control mechanisms required. The
computer represented a tool that was naturally designed
to easily perform this switching function. It is in
this manner that the two technologies complement and
support one another--communications facilities are
used to expand and extend the capabilities of computers;
computers are used to control and expand communications
systems.[38]

There are also strong economic and social
influences promoting increased cooperation between
telecommunications and computer interests. It is
important to recognize that this cooperation represents
far more than a scattering of technical improvements.
There has been a fundamental change in the scope and
utility of all our resources for gathering, exchanging
and using information.[39] Schiller has labeled today's
telecommunications technology as one of the most
dynamic forces, affecting not only the ideological
but the material bases of society.[40] With the broad

---

[38] Ibid.

[39] Robert L. Werner, "A Lawyer Looks at Our
Communications Policy," Jurimetrics Journal, 11
(December, 1970), p. 81.

[40] Herbert I. Schiller, Mass Communications
and American Empire (New York: Augustus M. Kelly
Publishers, 1971), p. 33.

implementation of "distributed computer" concepts, the usefulness of interactive, automated information processing systems can be further extended to the general populace on a shared basis.[41]

b. Computercations

The term "computercations" has been proffered here not just to keep the etymologist of tomorrow employed but rather to specifically indicate an intimate relationship between the computer and communications disciplines. This is not meant to imply simply the tying of a telephone to a computer, but rather the distribution of computation functions throughout a medium of communications, to any or all terminal points.[42]

Computers became linked with communications services at the Massachusetts Institute of Technology with the inauguration of Project MAC in 1961, which is believed to be the initial mating of communications and computers. It was now possible for the user to reach the computer from remote locations via communications channels furnished by common carriers and to thereby have on-line and real-time access to the

---

[41]Taub, "FCC Regulation of Domestic Computer Communications: A Competitive Reform," p. 949.

[42]A "distributed" computing system can either take the form of remote input devices interconnected to a central processor, or the addition of intelligent terminals, or interconnected computers.

computer as well as instantaneous response from it.[43]

Several major technological developments have fostered this increasingly close relationship between data processing and communications. One major break-through was the development of input-output devices, called terminals, that could be used to transmit and receive data (to and from a computer) at a remote location via the common carriers' facilities. However, an initial shortcoming of computer systems was that they were capable of processing only one job at a time. Time-sharing technology, where new hardware and software enabled third-generation computers to process several jobs simultaneously, significantly altered this situation.[44]

Digital transmission is undoubtedly one of the more significant developments effecting the conversation of machines. Computers "talk" in digital mode--a series of "on" and "off" pulses. Most conventional communications systems transmit in analog format--a continuous wave-like signal. Noise and interference, as well as signal, are amplified in the process of transmission. A listener can screen out such unwanted noise but a machine cannot. For computercations,

---

[43]Strassburg, "Communications and Computers: How Shall the Twain Meet?", p. 70.

[44]Notes, "The FCC Computer Inquiry: Interfaces of Competitive and Regulated Markets," Michigan Law Review, 71 (November, 1972), pp. 173-174.

transmission accuracy becomes much more critical.
Digital transmission provides just such performance
and the requirement of modems, which are translation
devices that convert digital outputs to analog
formats for transmission over conventional networks,
is eliminated and along with it a great deal of
expense and a potential source of error.[45] Another
benefit of a digital system is reduced costs. Digital
technology can squeeze more messages into each
circuit, thus reducing costs by improving transmission
efficiency.

The combination of rapidly advancing technology
and vigorous competition in the computer industry has
decreased the cost of computer time. Consequently,
as computation costs have fallen, communications costs
have become more and more significant.[46] Lawrence
Roberts of Telenet Communications and formerly with
the Office of the Secretary of Defense's Advanced
Research Projects Agency estimates that the crossover
point, where the cost of using computers to allocate
bandwidth [time sharing the frequencies by means of
computer switching] became cheaper than the cost of
the communications themselves, occurred during 1969.[47]

---

[45]Wynn Walters, "Computer Communications: The
Start of a Revolution," The Business Quarterly
(Winter, 1973), p. 83.

[46]Notes, "The FCC Computer Inquiry," p. 175.

[47]Lawrence G. Roberts, "Data by the Packet,"
IEEE Spectrum (February, 1974), pp. 46-51.

Bernard Strassburg, Chief of the FCC's Common Carrier Bureau at the time, suggested that the common carrier communications industry was "functioning in the eye of a hurricane surrounded by unprecedented turbulence."[48] In 1900, there were few who could foresee the impact and implications of the Gibbs concept of describing the universe in terms of probabilities. Similarly today, it is equally unlikely that more than a handful of people fully perceive the full impact of the combining computers with telecommunications.[49]

We may speculate ad infinitum as to the possible applications to which computer technology may be put in the future. However, one thing is certain; a communications link will provide the means by which its potential will be fully realized.[50] In providing such links, the satellite's capabilities far surpassed

---

[48] Horace P. Moulton, "Monopoly and Competition Issues Facing the Communications Industries," The Antitrust Bulletin, 13 (Fall, 1968), p. 889.

[49] Stanley Winkler, "Computer Communication-- the Quiet Revolution," Computer Communication--Impacts and Implications, Stanley Winkler, editor, ACM/ICCC, 1972, p. 29. J. W. Gibbs (1839-1903) was a mathematical physicist who wrote of, among other things, the electromagnetic theory of light. His most important publication was his famous paper, "On the Equilibrium of Heterogeneous Substances." Only after engineering and physics had considered the science of distributions were the developments of modern communications possible.

[50] Strassburg, "Communications and Computers: How Shall the Twain Meet?", p. 70.

those of the existing terrestrial systems.

Business demands computercations. With their enormous appetites for information, computers can collect, assemble and analyze vast amounts of information and give managers the data they need. Telecommunications gets the information where it is needed, when it is needed and in the form it is needed. As computers and telecommunications become even more inseparable in the future, the delineation between the processing function, the switching function, and the transmission function will become increasingly blurred. In a digital network, computers will take on the appearance of "fat spots" of data in the transmission links.[51] In an FCC public inquiry on computers and communications, initiated in 1966 and extending to 1971, specific attention was focused on these growing interrelationships.

c. The Computer Inquiry

Within the same year that the question of domestic satellite communications was raised, the basic definition of communications was also being questioned as a result of technological trends. On November 10, 1966 the Commission launched the Computer Inquiry to explore the broad range of regulatory and policy problems generated by these technological

---

[51]Walters, "Computer Communications," p. 81.

developments.[52] While some observers believed that
the giant strides made in the technologies of computer
components and telecommunications would inevitably
lead to a "total computer telecommunication" utility,[53]
the threshold question of the inquiry was namely, where
was the "line of demarcation" between communications
and data processing?[54] The questions posed by the
Inquiry and the subsequent responses and replies ranged
from consideration of the current and future trends
relating to the computer and information processing
industry; to the adequacy of existing legislation to
deal with such trends; to the need for new measures
"to protect the privacy and proprietary nature of
data. . .transmitted over communication facilities. . ."[55]

Over 3000 pages of material were submitted from
the communications industry, the data processing
industry, common carriers, users, government and

---

[52]7 FCC 2d 11, Docket No. 16979, Regulatory
and Policy Problems Presented by the Interdependence
of Computer and Communication Services and Facilities,
1966.

[53]Robert A. Dunlop, "The Emerging Technology
of Information Utilities," The Information Utility
and Social Change (Montvale, New Jersey: AFIPS
Press, 1970), p. 45.

[54]Strassburg, "Communications and Computers:
How Shall the Twain Meet?", p. 73.

[55]Robert E. Lee, "The Role of the Federal
Communications Commission," Computer Communications--
Impacts and Implications, ACM/ICCC, 1972, p. 49.

other interested parties. An explanation of the

categories of systems that were discussed is necessary

for an understanding of the growing computer/communica-

tion relationships:

    (1)   Data processing--the use of a computer
         for the processing of information as
         distinguished from circuit or message
         switching. Processing involves the use
         of the computer for functions such as
         storing, retrieving, sorting, merging
         and calculating data according to pro-
         grammed instructions.

    (2)   Message switching--the computer-controlled
         transmission of messages between two or
         more points via communications facilities
         wherein the content of the message remains
         unaltered. The Commission has specifically
         excluded this from the data processing
         category.

    (3)   Hybrid data processing--a service
         offering wherein the message-switching
         capability is incidental to the data
         processing function of purpose.

    (4)   Hybrid communications--a service
         offering wherein the data processing
         capability is incidental to the
         message-switching function or purpose.[56]

Although the continual development of the computerca-

tions technology makes classification difficult and

while the distinction between message switching and

data processing loses validity in direct proportion

to the sophistication and complexity of the computer

hardware and software, these categories are the best

definitions currently available for this discussion.[57]

---

[56]Notes, "The FCC Computer Inquiry," pp. 178-179.

[57]Delbert D. Smith, "The Interdependence of
Computer and Communications Services and Facilities:

The FCC's primary interest was with the communications common carriers; theirs was a regulated market which operated under tariffs, schedules of rates and charges. The dynamic computer industry represented the competitive market; driven by innovation and free enterprise. The line between hybrid communications and hybrid data processing thus was important because it marked the boundary between tariffed and nontariffed services.[58] The distinction between hybrid services was subtle and it became more complex with each technical innovation. The most obvious form of hybrid communications function performed by a computer is store-and-forward message switching, in which the computer acts as an intermediary between the sender and the receiver.[59]

There were three groups of competitors [and still are] that could influence the future of the data processing field--the computer industry, the service bureau industry (which performs data processing

---

A Question of Federal Regulation," University of Pennsylvania Law Review, 117 (April, 1969), p. 831.

[58]The Bell System is precluded from offering nontariffed services by its 1956 consent decree. In addition, Bell spokesmen have consistently disavowed any intent to compete in the field of computer manufacture or data processing service. See Strassburg, "Competition and Monopoly in the Computer and Data Transmission Industries," The Antitrust Bulletin, 13 (Fall, 1968), p. 993.

[59]Notes, "The FCC Computer Inquiry," p. 183.

on a fee or contract basis and includes specialized
subscription services) and the communications common
carriers. As the data processing industry grew, it
approached "unprecedented intimacy" with the communications industry.[60] What provided specific appeal to
all was the market's potential. The number of data
terminals installed in the United States during 1970
was about 185,000 and was estimated to reach 2,500,000
by 1980. It was also anticipated that the number of
data transmissions per year would jump from almost 15
billion to 248 billion by the decade's end.[61] Today,
data transmission services comprise less than two percent
of the entire loading of any system (or approximately
two percent of the telephone traffic) but are estimated
to be growing at the rate of fifty percent per year.
It has been estimated that by 1984 as much as ninety
percent of the computers used in the United States will
be tied into the public communications system.[62]

In their Inquiry comments to the Commission

---

[60]Notes, "The FCC Computer Inquiry," pp. 176,
181, 187.

[61]Taub, "FCC Regulation of Domestic Computer
Communications," p. 950. See Nolan, "Moving Business
Data is Big Business," Rutgers Journal of Computers
and Law, 1 (Fall, 1970), pp. 2, 4.

[62]Ibid., p. 949; see also Computers and Telecommunications, Organization for Economic Cooperation
and Development Information Studies, 3 (Paris: OECD,
1973), p. 11. Also noted again by R. E. Butler, note
63, infra, p. 50.

concerning the adequacy of the then available data
transmission services, by and large some sixty
respondents--with the exception of the common carriers--
were critical of the service offerings then being
provided. One of the larger problems that faced both
the computer and communications industries was the
lack of advanced communications capabilities in computer
systems [to a large extent this remains a significant
problem today].[63] The computercation requirements
demanded digital transmission facilities with greater
efficiencies. Quality, speed, capacity and economy,
the kind of improvements that a satellite system could
provide, were noted to be lacking.

IBM, in its response, commented:

Data communications requirements
have been met to date by adaptation
of facilities designed primarily
for voice services. While there
are important advantages in using
a single network, there are fundamental differences in the requirements of voice and data communications.

Bunker-Ramo Corporation observed:

The existing costs of communications
channels and facilities within the
present tariff structure are an
inhibiting factor to the widespread
use of computer services.

Sanders Associates, Inc., a defense contractor
and manufacturer believed that:

---

[63]R. E. Butler, "International Cooperation and
Regulation--Foundations for Development," _Telecommuni-_
cations, 10 (January, 1976), p. 53.

> . . .our existing colossally complex
> telephone network, while manifestly
> indispensable for voice transmission,
> cannot economically be transformed
> into an efficient data transmission
> medium.

Martin Marietta Corporation, a diversified aerospace manufacturer, noted:

> . . .requirements of data communica-
> tions must ultimately. . .be
> accommodated by specialized all-digital
> systems which. . .shall: (1) offer
> improved quality of data transmission,
> (2) provide faster access time, (3)
> provide higher bit rates [data rates]. . .

After considering such comments and various market studies, the FCC and its staff concluded that there was, in fact, public need for the proposed services and facilities, and noted that there was a large potential market yet to be developed.[64]

The Commission's Final Decision on the Computer Inquiry included the statement that: ". . .we are not proposing, at this time, to regulate data processing, as such, ..." However, because of the growing interdependence between the computer and the communications industry and the need to insure appropriate regulatory treatment, the Commission did recognize that

---

[64]Stuart L. Mathison and Philip M. Walker, "Regulatory Policy and Future Data Transmission Services," Computer Communications Networks (Englewood Cliffs, New Jersey: Prentice-Hall, Inc., 1973), pp. 342-344. Mathison and Walker also provide excellent coverage of the Computer Inquiry issues in Computers and Telecommunications, Chapter I, note 14.

there was a definite need for a maximum separation of activities which are subject to regulation from nonregulated activities involving data processing.[65] Although the Commission saw "no need to assert regulatory authority over data processing activities whether or not such services employ communications facilities in order to link the terminals of subscribers to centralized computers," it did retain the prerogative to "reexamine the policies set forth. . .if there should develop significant changes in the structure of the data processing industry."[66]

The Final Decision had not answered the question raised by the Justice Department regarding the Commission's jurisdictional authority. In its response to the Inquiry, Justice had concluded:

> It is our opinion that remote-access data processing is not common carrier communications and hence is not subject to the Commission's jurisdiction under Title II of the Communications Act.

The Commission, in concluding that regulation was unwarranted, had bypassed for the moment the question of whether or not it had the necessary legal authority to impose regulatory controls upon these services.

---

[65]Lee, "The Role of the Federal Communications Commission," p. 49.

[66]Stuart L. Mathison and Philip Walker, "Regulatory and Economic Issues of Computer Communications," Proceedings of the IEEE, 60 (November, 1972), p. 1257.

But in its decision it did conclude that it had "ample jurisdiction" to specify conditions under which common carriers may provide data processing services. The "line" became increasingly more difficult to define.[67] In the "hybrid service" area the Commission adopted a "wait-and-see" attitude, deciding that it did not have the Solomon-like wisdom needed to separate hybrid communications from hybrid data processing, and planned to treat such services on a case-by-case basis [in order that it might see how such systems would develop].[68] The Commission's decision, to regulate hybrid communications on a discretionary basis, as a practical matter, precluded data processing firms from offering such service because of the threat of regulation.[69]

One lesson that strongly emerged from the Inquiry was that the Commission henceforth would be concerned with the interdependence of two areas affecting our society, computers and communications.[70] Also decreasing computation costs, in conjunction with the fact that

---

[67]Ibid. Marcus Cohn, a former FCC lawyer, reviewed the Inquiry (see Rutgers Journal of Computers and Law, 1 (Fall, 1970)) in an article titled, "The Federal Communications Commission," to make the point.

[68]Lee, "The Role of the Federal Communications Commission," p. 50.

[69]Notes, "The FCC Computer Inquiry," p. 182.

[70]Lee, "The Role of the Federal Communications Commission," p. 50.

voice telephone lines have only a limited capacity
to handle data, would make any superior alternative
communications system, like a domestic satellite, a
welcome addition in the computer world.[71] But while
the computer-communications explosion was real and
accelerating, its full potential depended greatly on
communications developments like the satellite which,
while clearly visible, had yet to be broadly accomplished.[72]

3. The "New Competition"

When the Commission issued its Above 890
decision in 1959, it was by no means prepared to authorize
any additional competition in the common-carrier
communication business and made it clear that the door
was only open to individual users who wish to meet their
own individual needs.[73] However, the new wave of
regulatory activity, which started in 1968 and opened
up areas of common carrier service to competition, had
a substantial impact on the formulation of the DOMSAT
policy.[74] It put to the test of contemporary

---

[71]Taub, "FCC Regulation of Domestic Computer
Communications," p. 960.

[72]Dorff, "Computers and Communications," p. 22.

[73]Alfred E. Kahn, The Economics of Regulation:
Principles and Institutions, Vol. II (New York: John
Wiley and Sons, 1971), p. 131.

[74]Letter from Mr. Andrew Margeson, Staff
Economist, House of Representatives, Committee on
Interstate and Foreign Commerce, to Robert S. Magnant,
April 29, 1976. Dr. Manley Irwin, a former FCC

reasonableness the long-standing policies and practices of both the carriers and the Commission. It altered long-established institutional structures and conventions and opened the market place to the innovators; not only the innovators of electronic equipment but also the innovators of regulatory policy. Mr. Fred W. Henck, the editor of TELECOMMUNICATIONS REPORTS who has watched the industry's evolution for the past 35 years, sees the DOMSAT policy as a direct outgrowth of the Commission's interconnection and specialized carrier policies, both of which were developed while DOMSAT was pending.[75] This is also supported by Barry Taub in a 1973 article who referred to Carterfone (the interconnect policy) as the beginning of a second wave of competition which culminated in DOMSAT, "where the seeds planted by Above 890 began to flower."[76] Summaries of the interconnect and specialized carrier issues follow. These rulings made the integration of satellite systems with terrestrial networks possible.

---

economist, has identified DOMSAT as part of the Commission's new pro-competitive policy trend that was embarked upon in 1968. See Letter from Professor Manley R. Irwin, University of New Hampshire, to Robert S. Magnant, May 13, 1976.

[75]Letter from Mr. Fred W. Henck, Editor, TELECOMMUNICATIONS REPORTS, to Robert S. Magnant, May 17, 1976.

[76]Taub, "Federal Communications Commission Regulation of Domestic Computer Communications," pp. 966-970.

a. Interconnection

The Communications Act of 1934 specifically
provided for the protection of the nation's telecommunications common carriers from outside competition
through regulation as was noted in Chapter I. But in
the strict sense this was not meant to be an eternal
umbrella for the common carriers. A changing of the
environment began almost twenty years ago; thoughts of
private systems, foreign attachments and specialized
services gave birth to the interconnection issue.

In recent years the question of interconnect,
which includes not only the interconnection of
subscriber-provided terminal devices, but also of
independent communications systems (such as a domestic
satellite system) to the telephone network, has
generated considerable controversy. Historically,
the telephone companies prohibited such interconnection
by their subscribers, maintaining that it might
jeopardize the telephone network if uncontrolled, but
also recognizing that it would most certainly cut into
the sales of their manufacturing subsidiaries (such as
AT&T's Western Electric and GT&E's Automatic Electric).[77]

The carrier's arguments of potential system
harm were generally accepted without question by the
and the state public-utility commissions in the past

---

[77]Mathison and Walker, "Regulatory and Economic
Issues of Computer Communications," p. 1260.

and consequently a seemingly impregnable wall was built around the telephone networks. However, the FCC's 1968 Carterfone decision caused the wall to crumble. Although Carterfone caused the most dramatic changes in interconnection regulation, it wasn't its beginning. Over a decade earlier the common carriers' blanket prohibition against interconnection of customer-owned equipment was tested before the U.S. Court of Appeals, in Hush-a-Phone Corporation v. United States.[78] This case concerned a rubber cuplike device designed to be attached to the microphone portion of the telephone handset to provide privacy in conversation; its use on the Nation's telephone network had been barred by provisions in the carrier's tariffs. Reviewing the Bell interstate toll tariff, the court found the ban to be illegal and ruled that it was ". . .an unwarranted interference with the telephone subscriber's right to use his telephone

---

[78]99 U.S. App. D.C. 190, 238 F 2d 266, D.C. Cir. (1956). Actually the question of interconnect was raised almost 30 years ago! See 11 FCC 1033, Docket No. 6787, In the Matter of Use of Recording Devices in Connection with Telephone Service. Telephone recording devices have been in use to some extent since 1916 (Edison, Inc. developed an acoustically coupled device in 1915 called the Telescribe). In its March 24, 1947 ruling the Commission found:

> insofar as any tariff regulations on file with us have the effect of barring such use of recording devices, such tariff regula-
> tions are unjust and unreasonable and therefore unlawful under the provision of section 201 of [the] Communications Act.

in ways which are privately beneficial without being publicly detrimental."[79]

AT&T was ordered by the court to revise its tariff to permit use of the Hush-a-Phone device. It did as ordered but the revised tariff retained the general interconnection prohibition. Consequently, in 1966, Carter Electronics Corporation brought an antitrust suit against the Bell System and GT&E of the Southwest.[80] The case was referred to the FCC. The Carterfone was an electronic device used for acoustically coupling the base station of a mobile radio system (or other private communication system) with the telephone network.[81] The telephone companies argued before the FCC that use of the Carterfone violated the integrity of the telephone system, which required the use of carrier-supplied attachments only. The Commission was not persuaded by this argument and in a unanimous opinion, in June 1969, found the tariff restrictions to be unreasonable, unlawful and discriminatory under the Communications Act of 1934.

The Commission further concluded:

---

[79]Ibid.

[80]Mathison and Walker, "Regulatory and Economic Issues of Computer Communication," p. 1261.

[81]Approximately 3500 of these devices were sold between 1959 and 1966. The telephone companies warned Carter's customers that the tariffs prohibited such devices and those who violated them risked having their telephone service terminated.

> . . .a customer desiring to use an
> interconnecting device to improve
> the utility to him of both the
> telephone system and a private radio
> system should be able to do so, so
> long as the interconnection does not
> adversely affect the telephone company's
> operations or the telephone system's
> utility for others. A tariff which
> prevents this is unreasonable; it is
> also unduly discriminatory where, as
> here, the telephone company's own
> interconnecting equipment is approved
> for use. The vice of the present
> tariff. . .is that it prohibits the
> use of harmless, as well as harmful
> devices.[82]

The Commission appropriately struck the unlawful tariff

and permitted the carriers to propose new tariff provi-

sions in accordance with its opinion and to specify

technical standard for the protection of the telephone

system against harmful devices if they so desired.

b.   The Specialized Carriers

The MCI and Specialized Carrier decisions were

extensions of the Above 890 decision. After the latter,

if you had a requirement for your own private

communications but you could not afford your own

private system, what the common carrier was offering

for services was all you could get. In 1963, Microwave

Communications, Inc. (MCI) recognized this fact and

petitioned the FCC for a license to offer "specialized

----

[82]Use of the Carterfone Device in Message Toll
Telephone Service, 13 FCC 2d 420 (1968), pp. 424-425.
Additional perspective on the impact of Carterfone is
found in Mathison and Walker, note 66, supra, pp.
1262-1264.

services." It took six years for MCI's construction permits to be approved but in 1969 the precedent was set for the establishment of new carriers, primarily because the established carriers [as previously noted in the responses of the Computer Inquiry] were not providing the user with the services that were wanted.[83]

MCI went on the air as a full-fledged specialized carrier on January 1, 1972. If that were all that had happened, there would be little cause for more than academic interest in the "computercations" community. However, the FCC's 1969 approval of MCI's permits triggered over 1900 new microwave station applications from several dozen firms who were proposing to build new specialized-carrier facilities. One of the applicants, the Data Transmission Company (Datran) proposed to build a nation-wide, all-digital, switched network and offer exclusively data-transmission services on both a switched and private-line basis.[84]

These numerous and varied applications presented the FCC with a major policy problem, for the Commission was not sure that its MCI precedent should be extended on a nationwide basis without further analysis.

---

[83]Mathison and Walker, "Regulatory and Economic Issues of Computer Communication," pp. 1264-1266. A variety of dedicated private-line services (data services, or a combination of data and voice) in truth was more than the existing carriers were willing to provide or, in some cases, capable of providing.

[84]Ibid., pp. 1264-1265.

Therefore, in July 1970, it issued a public inquiry into the merits of the specialized-carrier concept (Docket No. 18920). As might have been expected from previous experience in the Computer Inquiry, the question elicited strong support for the MCI and Datran concepts from all sections, with the exception of the established carriers, of course.[85]

The Commission opted in favor of the specialized-carrier concept in order to obtain the new services and to stimulate better performance of the existing carriers. Its decision of May 1971 [Specialized Carrier] permitted virtually free entry of all financially and technically qualified applicants into the specialized carrier service, and it denied a joint petition by the National Association of Regulatory Utility Commissioners (NARUC) and the Utilities and Transportation Commission of the State of Washington (WUTC), for reconsideration of the specialized common carrier concept.[86] With the assistance of the Commission, competition was being established and the FCC could be expected to reject tariffs submitted by the established carriers which would tend to drive out their new competitors.[87]

[85]Ibid., p. 1267.

[86]U.S. Superintendent of Documents, 38th Annual Report/Fiscal Year 1972, Federal Communications Commission (Washington, D.C.: Government Printing Office), stock no. 0480-00271, p. 99.

[87]Stuart L. Mathison and Philip M. Walker, "Specialized Common Carriers," Telephone Engineering and Management (October 15, 1971), p. 58.

As late as May, 1974, however, the Commission was required to intercede in behalf of the specialized carriers [MCI in this case] and direct AT&T to provide interconnect services, which AT&T was attempting to deny (through subtle legal machinations) in its continuing fight to minimize the effects of the new carriers.[88] The Commission also placed all telephone companies on notice that its policy declarations applied to them as well as to Bell and emphasized that it expected compliance.[89]

In January, 1975, a three-judge tribunal of the U.S. Court of Appeals, in a unanimous decision, affirmed that the FCC had properly exercised its "broad" and "sweeping" authority in common carrier regulation to produce its specialized common carrier policy. This decision concluded the appeal that had been filed by NARUC/WUTC challenging the FCC's denial of its earlier petition. Judge Browning noted that the Commission's authority had been specifically stated broadly "to meet the needs of a dynamic rapidly changing industry."[90] While the telephone companies

---

[88]"AT&T Loses Motion: Will Reconnect MCI's Private-Line Services," Wall Street Journal (May 3, 1974), 17:4. Also see WSJ 1/4, 19:1; 2/19, 17:1; and 4/24, 15:1.

[89]"FCC Gives Green Light to Specialized Common Carriers," Microwaves (June, 1974), p. 24. An MCI official was quoted as saying, "It was a breached delivery, but at least we're born."

[90]"FCC Properly Exercised 'Broad' and 'Sweeping'

opposed this competition, they also recognized the inevitability in its development as was indicated by the nature of their responses and their various tariff revisions.[91]

Although the factors identified thus far were influencing both the regulated and the regulator during DOMSAT, there were additional influences on the regulator. They were to be found within the government structure and were evident during two separate administrations.

B. The Policy Makers

The influences that the Eisenhower and Kennedy administrations had on DOMSAT were manifested in the Communications Satellite Act of 1962, which laid the foundations for DOMSAT. But both the Johnson and Nixon administrations would play major roles before the DOMSAT policy was finalized, and an assortment of personalities would participate.[92] In technical

---

Powers," Telecommunications Reports, Vol. 41, No. 4, (January 27, 1975), pp. 6-9. Keller and Heckman, Telecommunications counsel for the National Retail Merchants Association, appeared before the San Francisco Court of Appeals to argue in favor of upholding the Commission's decision. See W. H. Borghesani, Jr., "The Evolving Telecommunications Regulatory Environment-- Parts I and II," Telephone Interconnect Journal (November, 1973-January, 1974), pp. 20-22, 31 and pp. 22-24.

[91]Letter from Henck, May 17, 1976.

[92]Appendix B provides a picture in time of the relationships that existed between prime participants in DOMSAT.

circles the extent of political participation in policy making is well recognized, as was so aptly put by the editors of a recent technical society publication:

> The technical solutions to problems
> presented by user needs are constrained
> or inspired just as much (if not more)
> by economics and the impact of conflict-
> ing societal pressures (as embodied in
> regulatory decision) as by the cleverness
> or lack of cleverness of the engineer.[93]

From 1965 to 1968, the White House, under the Johnson Administration, turned its attention toward a review of the Nation's telecommunications policy. The President's Task Force on Communications Policy, appointed in 1967 and supported by the FCC, the National Academy of Engineering and others conducted extensive reviews of both policy and technology in a variety of areas with considerable emphasis on DOMSAT.[94] It recommended that a COMSAT-directed pilot program be authorized for domestic satellite, since at that time the potential benefits were too indeterminate to permit an informed decision as to how such satellites might best be utilized "in the public interest."[95]

---

[93]Paul E. Green, Jr. and Robert W. Lucks (eds.), Computer Communications (New York: IEEE Press, 1975), p. 4.

[94]Michael J. Morrissey and John J. Smith, "FCC Activities: Domestic Satellites", George Washington Law Review, 41 (May, 1973), pp. 746-759.

[95]President's Task Force on Communications Policy, Final Report (Washington, D.C.: U.S. Government Printing Office, 1969), Chapter 5, pp. 9-17.

However, in 1969, after a change in administrations,
the questions of ownership and operation were reexamined
and an "open entry" policy was recommended.

As noted in Chapter I, the Commission has the
responsibility of supervising schedules of charges
filed with it, for licensing new entrants, and for
issuing certificates of public convenience. The agency
can execute these functions by formulating policy
either through rulemaking or through adjudication.
Frequently the agency will issue a tentative decision
or proposed rulemaking which is open to comment by
interested parties to enable it to make an informed
final decision of policy.[96] Adjudication on the other
hand has been denoted as the agency process for
formulation of a formal order. Congress has conferred
on the U.S. Courts of Appeals jurisdiction to review
only the final orders of the Commission. It is not
uncommon to find reversed adjudicative proceedings,
but the agency's judgment regarding rulemaking has
seldom been disturbed.[97]

The purpose of the proposed rulemaking for
Docket No. 16495 was "to facilitate expeditious actions
on the applications [for DOMSAT systems] and prompt

---

[96]Taub, "Federal Communications Commission
Regulation of Domestic Computer Communications," p. 951.
Rulemaking is defined as the process of formulating,
amending or repealing a rule.

[97]Ibid., p. 952.

attainment of the potential benefits of the satellite
technology in the domestic field" and to keep open the
proceedings of the docket.[98] No cutoff date for the
filing of applications was established at that time.
With proposed filings submitted, the Commission would
then decide on the questions of policy presented.
The Commission invited all those who were legally,
technically and financially qualified, to file applications for satellite systems that proposed services
directly to the public on a common carrier basis, or
to other common carriers, or for a combination of
such arrangements.[99] At the same time, the Commission
also instituted a general rulemaking on the policies
to be followed in the event of technical or economic
conflicts between applications and on the initial
role of AT&T in DOMSAT, access to Earth stations, and
procurement policies.[100]

It would take two more rulings, a change of
administrations, and more than thirty-three months
before all matters were finally resolved.

1. Activities of the Johnson Administration

On August 14, 1967, President Lyndon B. Johnson,

---

[98]22 FCC 2d 86, Report and Order, FCC 70-306.
To be referred to as the First Report.

[99]Robert L. Werner, "A Lawyer Looks at our Communications Policy," Jurimetrics Journal, 11 (December,
1970), p. 89.

[100]22 FCC 2d 810, Notice of Proposed Rulemaking.

provided the following thoughts to the Congress in a
policy message:

> [T]he challenge is to communicate.
> No technological advance offers a
> greater opportunity for meeting this
> challenge than the alliance of space
> exploration and communication. Since
> the advent of the communications
> satellite, the linking of one nation
> to another is no longer dependent on
> telephone lines, microwaves or cables
> under the sea.[101]

He noted, "Communications satellites have domestic as
well as international applications," and asked the
Task Force, which he was appointing by this message,
to look at the Nation's overall communications policy
and to address the following two questions in its
primary efforts:

> --How soon will a domestic satellite system
>   be economically feasible?

> --Should a domestic satellite system be
>   general purpose or specialized and should
>   there be more than one system?

Additionally, the Task Force was to determine if either
the Communication Act of 1934 or the Communication
Satellite Act of 1962 required revision and to consider
the international aspects of communication satellites
and the utilization of the frequency spectrum.[102] It
was clear in his message that the potential impact of

---

[101]U.S. Congress, Message from the President of
the United States, House of Representatives, House
Document No. 157, 90th Congress, 1st Sess., August,
1967, p. 1.

[102]Ibid., pp. 5, 8, and 9.

the communications satellite on domestic policy was well recognized and that this was one of the major reasons that overall communications policy was being examined.

While much of Johnson's message was in an international context, it would have been unreasonable to expect that the domestic communications environment would remain static while the international environment exploded with this new technology. As Johnson said:

> Such an archaic system of international communications is no longer necessary. The communications satellite knows no geographic boundary, is dependent on no cable, owes allegiance to no single language or political philosophy. Man now has it within his power to speak directly to his fellow man in all nations.[103]

a. The Johnson Task Force

The Task Force was chaired by Eugene V. Rostow, the then Under Secretary of State for Political Affairs. On December 7, 1968, after more than fifteen months of policy examination, the Task Force [with the cooperation of fifteen departments and agencies of the Federal Government] issued its Final Report.[104]

---

[103]U.S. Congress, Message from the President, p. 4.

[104]Final Report, President's Task Force on Communications Policy, December 7, 1968 (Washington, D.C.: Government Printing Office, 1969), 0-351-636. Those involved were State, Defense, Justice, Commerce, Labor, HEW, HUD, Transportation, USIA, NASA, Bureau of the Budget, Council of Economic Advisors, Office of Science and Technology, National Aeronautics and Space Council and the Office of Telecommunications Management. The

Noteworthy was the fact that this Task Force had attempted the broadest review of national telecommunications ever undertaken; also that one of the most significant problems identified involved the efficient introduction of communications satellites into domestic service.

The Report's staff studies indicated that satellites would be competitive with terrestrial facilities in meeting some domestic communications requirements.[105] The economic practicality was no longer considered to be a question. The Report envisioned complementing "overlaid" networks but not revolutionizing the fabric of the existing terrestrial systems. The satellite's ability to reallocate communications capacity flexibly and rapidly among a number of individual routes [in other words, "variable capacity routes"] was seen in the Report as possibly "economically and operationally attractive" but impossible to evaluate.[106] Permitting the competitive market to do this was not even suggested. The Saturday Review noted in retrospect [1971] that:

> Some observers think that, in 1967,
> the FCC would have designated AT&T

FCC's participation was ex-officio in nature, necessary because of the Commission's statutory responsibility.

[105]Ibid., Chapter 5, p. 7.

[106]Ibid., pp. 5-6.

and COMSAT as the chosen entities
[for DOMSAT]. Authorization was
delayed pending the report of
President Johnson's Task Force. . .[107]

But the article provided no support for this observa-

tion. However, even if the observation was accurate,

the Task Force Report certainly didn't provide much

in the way of options for the Commission to consider.

The available data was believed to be insufficient.

Answering Johnson's questions of "how soon" and

"what kind", the Task Force sidestepped the issues by

noting that "a number of unresolved questions make it

premature to establish full-scale domestic satellite

operations at this time" and "substantial disagreement

also exists as to the comparative advantages of a

general purpose domestic satellite system and one or

more systems 'dedicated' to specialized uses. . . ."[108]

The Task Force concluded by advocating no more

than what the FCC was alleged to have been previously

considering, that a COMSAT pilot program should be

established first to gain insight. The Report noted:

> [W]hile our own independent estimates
> do not indicate that substantial
> economies will result in the very near
> term from the substitution of satellite
> facilities for a terrestrial equivalent,
> neither do they show that some uses of
> domestic satellites--particularly for

---

[107] Robert Lewis Shayon, "Bird Watching,"
Saturday Review, April 17, 1971, p. 57.

[108] Final Report, President's Task Force on
Communications Policy, Chapter 5, p. 9.

> television distribution--are bound
> to be uneconomical.[109]

With this statement both sides of the coin were covered.

In fairness, though, the general themes of the Report [the needs for more competition and greater innovation] can be considered positive and constructive. It recognized that the Commission had broad regulatory powers under both the 1934 and 1962 Acts and recommended that they be strengthened, by Congress if necessary, to cope with the rapidly changing technological environment and to insure effective regulation.[110]

While its technical projections were limited, the Report did provide the following observation on message switching in a footnote:

> When teleprocessing [computercations]
> moves into a separate digital network,
> with time division switching, economies
> of scale may become very strong.[111]

In the Report's dissenting statement, Vice-Chairman James D. O'Connell added emphasis to a point that was only lightly touched upon in the basic report. Expressing

---

[109]Ibid., pp. 17-18. ABC had made that same appraisal in 1965.

[110]Werner, "A Lawyer Looks at our Communications Policy," p. 81. Congress took no action in this area.

[111]Final Report, President's Task Force, Chapter 6, p. 33. Someone at IBM must have certainly read and pondered that thought for a while, as well as COMSAT, AT&T and many others. The Task Force, however, appeared to have no appreciation at that time for the potential of satellite technology or for the economies that digital technology could bring.

confidence in the regulatory process,[112] O'Connell

felt that the Executive Branch and the FCC could

initiate the necessary improvements called for in the

area of telecommunications policy. But he emphasized

that a substantial augmentation of the resources of

these offices would be necessary to accomplish these

improvements for the task was enormous.[113] Although

the Task Force Report was widely quoted, it was never

released officially, nor was it acted upon by either

the outgoing or the incoming administration.[114]

b. The National Academy of Engineering

Some of the technical considerations of DOMSAT

were investigated by the National Academy of Engineering

(NAE) and the results were furnished to the Task Force

in a separate report.[115] The NAE had been established

in 1964 to share in the responsibilities of the

---

[112]It must be kept in mind that the goals of
regulation and competition are identical--efficiency,
progressiveness, reasonable prices and satisfaction
of diverse needs. See Lionel Kestenbaum, "The Limits
of a Regulated Monopoly: Telephone Attachments,
Interconnections, and Use of Circuits," The Antitrust
Bulletin, 13 (1969), pp. 979, 983.

[113]Final Report, President's Task Force, Tab
B, pp. 7-9.

[114]David C. Acheson, "Domestic Satellite
Developments," Public Utilities Fortnightly, 86
(September 24, 1970), p. 68.

[115]Reports on Selected Topics in Telecommunications, The Final Report by the Committee on Telecommunications, National Academy of Engineering
(Washington, D.C.: National Academy of Sciences, 1969).

National Academy of Sciences. The Committee on
Telecommunications had been established in March
1968 to (1) undertake preliminary review and evaluation
of some of the reports of the Task Force and (2) to
act in an advisory capacity to the Task Force on
technical matters.[116] The NAE's intent was to contribute further understanding of selected problems in
order to encourage action towards their solution.
It was not concerned with organizational or jurisdictional considerations. Rate-policy considerations as
they affected the revenue to be expected from a given
set of communications facilities were also excluded.

The NAE compared satellite and terrestrial
systems, making observations on demand projections,
economic considerations and system designs. Because
of land cable improvements, the cost advantages of
microwave relay for large cross-section routes had
been disappearing since 1948. The leading candidates
for the larger cross-section land routes of the future
were millimeter-wave waveguide systems and laser
guided-beam systems. Both were extensions of the
land cable concept, being fully guided systems. In
making comparisons between alternative systems it is
important to realize that it was being done at a
particular instant in time for particular demand and

---

[116]Ibid., pp. 1-4.

technology predictions. Longer-range views require
that added attention be given to the uncertainty
that exists with respect to future developments.

For a realistic analysis, two specific
comparisons of satellites and cables were done, based
on a simplified model of long-haul transmission in the
Atlantic basin for the period 1968 to 1985, starting
with the 1967 demand projections of the Joint World
Plan Committee of the ITU.[117] It was found that all
new demand could be met with satellites, that such a
system would be a minimum cost system, that a premium
must be paid for the use of cables, and that cables
could be used to temporarily postpone an investment in
satellites for a year or two in certain cases.[118]

As seen by the NAE, the economic considerations
of a domestic satellite system tended to focus on the
calculation of a break-even distance above which the
satellite service would be cheaper than terrestrial
links. Domestic service meant the use of satellites
more or less within the boundaries of a particular
nation. The break-even distance is influenced
strongly by the extent of terrestrial facilities

---

[117]International Telecommunication Union, Joint
World Plan Committee of the CCIR and CCITT, General
Plan for the Development of Interregional Telecommunication Network, 1967-1970-1975 (Geneva: ITU, 1968;
meeting held in Mexico City, 1967).

[118]Reports on Selected Topics in Telecommunications, pp. 5-8, 13.

already in existence at the time the new satellite
service is contemplated. Break-even distance is a
complex function of the total traffic handled and the
number of routes to be served (route traffic density).
The space segment cost of a satellite system is almost
independent of whether the total traffic capacity of
the satellite is used in connecting a high traffic-
density route or in interconnecting many points with
lower traffic density. In the latter type system the
break-even distance could be lower than in the former
but Earth station costs are a critical factor. The
problem would be simplified if the only factors
involved were careful forecasts of the service requirements and the economic optimization of the technical
approach. However, matters of national prestige, policy
determination regarding the scope and purpose of
service, and political influence were also in the
picture and had to be taken into consideration and
included in the NAE's report.[119]

The NAE recognized that satellite systems had
a distinct cost advantage over undersea cable and
provided flexible low-cost service through multiple-
access capabilities. Because of this, if traffic
demands were small, the alternative of sharing the
international satellite with domestic traffic clearly

-----

[119] Ibid., pp. 21-22.

offered the most economic solution. On the other hand,
if traffic demand was large (thousands of channels)
a separate satellite was thought to be more practical.
However, satellite design (to include replacement and
growth-in-capacity considerations) could be more
effectively optimized if only domestic service was to
be provided. One result of rather conservative
technology forecasts throughout the study was that
costs-per-channel of the systems compared were thought
to be reasonably correct for 1980 even though the actual
technology in that time period may be different from
what was projected.[120] The satellite technology
available (as seen by the Academy) offered attractive
prospects for domestic communication services on either
a modest scale or on a large scale and new types of
service which would otherwise be impractical would
"no doubt lead to very serious consideration of this
type of facility."[121]

2. A Change of Administrations

As Presidents changed, so did perspectives on
policy. The FCC took no action on the domestic satellite

---

[120]Ibid., pp. 19-20, 23. In the DOMSAT filings,
there would be applications for 24 orbit slots, but
four of these were designated for ground spares. Even
with Canada's proposed satellites included, all
systems could be accommodated on an individual basis.

[121]Ibid., pp. 25-26.

issue while waiting for an expression of opinion from the new Administration.[122] Indications that the Task Force Report was unacceptable to the new Nixon Administration and that the White House would support an intensive reexamination of national telecommunications policy (and the implied postures toward competition and regulation in the communications industry) had been in the air since Nixon's election in 1968.[123]

In testimony before the House Subcommittee on Communications on March 6, 1969, Congress had been made aware of the lack of activity on the DOMSAT issue and the Final Report of the Rostow group. The FCC's Chairman Rosel Hyde noted:

> We deferred reaching any policy decisions in our domestic satellite inquiry pending conclusion of the work of the President's Task Force on Communications Policy [Rostow's Task Force]. . .Our staff likewise participated in discussions and in my judgment was very helpful in providing information to the task force. So, we are conversant with their deliberations, notwithstanding the fact that the report which was submitted to the Chief Executive has not been released.[124]

---

[122]Acheson, "Domestic Satellite Developments," p. 68.

[123]Thomas P. Murphy, "Federal Regulatory Policy and Communications Satellites: Investing the Social Dividend," The American Journal of Economics and Sociology, 31 (October, 1972), p. 340.

[124]U.S. Congress, House, Subcommittee on Communications and Power, First Session on the Jurisdiction and Activities of the Federal Communications Commission, 91 Congress, March 6, 1969, pp. 3-4.

When the subcommittee's Chairman, Torbert Macdonald,

inquired as to the whereabouts of Rostow's study,

Hyde replied:

> It is my understanding that the
> Chairman of the task force, which
> was Mr. Rostow, transmitted the
> report to the President. This
> would be President L. B. Johnson
> and I presume it would have been
> transmitted from his administration
> to the new administration. . .I
> believe it was in November but
> I can get the date for you.[125]

The following information was submitted for the record

in the hearing report:

> The date of the letter of trans-
> mittal of the President's Task
> Force Report on Telecommunications
> was December 7, 1968.

There were new forces at work in the White House

and the questions of satellite communications policy

were being escalated to the highest macropolitical

level. A small working group was formulating

"Administration suggestions" regarding the introduction

of communications satellites into U.S. domestic com-

munications. A White House announcement, dated July

22, 1969 stressed: "We will be concerned, of course,

with the general structure and direction of the industry

and not with specific applications pending before the

Commission." Among the membership of this working

group was special Presidential staff assistant, Dr.

---

[125]Ibid.

Clay T. Whitehead.[126] The lucrative aspect of the
DOMSAT market seemed to draw interest also. As
COMSAT President Joseph V. Charyk observed:

> I think the very success of satel-
> lites for international application
> has complicated the problem of
> authorization on the domestic scene,
> because with the international success,
> it would appear that satellites are a
> good thing, and so everyone wants to
> get into the act domestically.[127]

With the release of a January 23, 1970 Memorandum from
Presidential Assistant Peter Flanigan to the new FCC
Chairman Dean Burch, the Nixon interest in DOMSAT
was confirmed:

> Federal policy on domestic satellite
> communications has been long delayed. . .
> At this stage of domestic satellite
> planning, it is not possible to
> identify major economies of scale.
> Rather, it appears that a diversity
> of multiple-satellite systems as
> well as multiple-earth stations will
> be required to provide a full range
> of domestic services.
>
> Further we find no public interest
> grounds for establishing a monopoly
> in domestic satellite communications.

It disagreed with the Task Force Report, recommending an "open skies" policy:

> Government policy should encourage
> and facilitate the development of

---

[126]Kurt Borchardt, Structure and Performance of
the U.S. Communications Industry (Boston: Harvard
University Press, 1970), pp. 129-130.

[127]Murphy, "Federal Regulatory Policy," p. 344;
see also House Report No. 859, Assessment of Space
Communications Technology, note 131 infra.

commercial domestic satellite
communication systems to the extent
private enterprise finds them
economically and operationally
feasible.[128]

a. The Commission

Although the FCC announced its Proposed Rulemaking and First Report on DOMSAT less than sixty

days after this memo was released, it should not be

quickly interpreted as a direct reaction to the

Flanigan memorandum, for the people on the Commission

at the time were not the type to jump at an Executive

dictate, particularly Nicholas Johnson, a veteran

Commissioner since 1966 who was known for speaking

his mind. He had described the period following the

Carterfone decision in the following manner:

> We haven't the slightest notion
> where we're going (or, indeed,
> even where we want to go)--but we
> know we're getting there a whole
> lot faster than before.[129]

He paints a slightly different picture of the DOMSAT

atmosphere at the time. Just one week prior to the

---

[128]22 FCC 2d 0125, The White House, Memorandum
for the Honorable Dean Burch, Chairman of the Federal
Communication Commission, January 23, 1970.

[129]Nicholas Johnson, "Harnessing Revolution: The
Role of Regulation and Competition for the Communications Industries of Tomorrow," The Antitrust Bulletin,
13 (Fall, 1968), p. 881. Johnson has been described by
Dr. Thomas Murphy as "a man who must seem inscrutable
to some while appearing most open and logical to
others. As one who champions the public interest, he
has made powerful enemies in the industry." See note
123, supra, p. 342.

First Report, Johnson was quoted:

> [I]n the summer of 1969 the Nixon
> Administration asked the FCC to
> delay once again while another
> Executive Department review was
> undertaken.[130]

A House Report on space communications also indicates
that the FCC was on the verge of announcement in its
decision regarding the domestic [satellite] system
about July 1969, when an additional delay was brought
about by an announcement that the White House had
established still another task force, chaired by Clay
T. Whitehead, to further review policy on domestic
satellite service.[131]

The Flanigan memorandum was interpreted by some
observers as signalling a conscious effort on the part
of the Executive to take a more forceful initiative
in planning and advocating measures that fall within
the purview of the regulatory agencies.[132] Speaking

---

[130]Remarks by Nicholas Johnson, March 12, 1970,
"The Capacity to Govern: The Role of the FCC in the
Development of National Policy for Computer Communica-
tions," Hopkins-Brooking Lecture Series, Computer
Communications and the Public Interest, Advanced
International Studies.

[131]U.S. Congress, House, Committee on Science
and Astronautics, Assessment of Space Communications
Technology, H. Rept. No. 859, March 3, 1970, 91st
Congress, 2nd Session, p. 19. The report concluded that
DOMSAT had not been inhibited thus far by industry
institutions [COMSAT had been advocating a domestic
satellite for the U.S. for almost 4 years (p. 4)].
There was no assessment as to whether government
institutions had hindered DOMSAT.

[132]Acheson, "Domestic Satellite Developments,"
p. 68.

before the American Bar Association in August 1970,

COMSAT's General Council, David C. Acheson, saw the

memo this way:

> [O]ne may wonder whether the January
> 23rd memorandum represents a truly
> sophisticated view of the domestic
> satellite question. "Competition" is
> an attractive word, but not every
> policy carrying the name is necessarily
> the real goods, union-made, preshrunk
> and Sanforized. For the near future
> there are probably only two uses of
> domestic satellite that would support
> the large requisite investment: They
> are the domestic telephone network
> and commercial broadcast distribution. . .[133]

At the FCC both old forces and new forces

were at work. Besides the "public interest" minded

Johnson, there was the Common Carrier Bureau's Bernard

Strassburg, its chief since 1964, a veteran of more

than twenty-five years with the Commission, and one

who had for years recognized the importance of data

transmission.

The Commission also had a new boss, Dean Burch.

Burch, the first Republican to chair the Commission

in nearly a decade, was also a strong advocate of the

public interest. He and Johnson, his most flamboyant

democratic colleage, contributed much to the formulation

of DOMSAT policy. With the appointment of Burch as

---

[133]Ibid. Even COMSAT had not recognized the
potential of the computercations market, even though
it had small processors conversing via satellite at
the time. See the discussion of SPADE in Network
Developments, Chapter IV.

Chairman the pace of activity and interest picked up considerably.[134]   Burch, who ran the 1964 presidential campaign of Barry Goldwater, was known as a champion of free enterprise, a "laissez faire" capitalist who would let the marketplace regulate communications. His detractors called him a "reckless intellectual hipshooter" and believed him to be "a bit rash".[135] One of the political people, he is listed as a Conservative from Arizona, but he is considered much broader and smarter than the connotations of any label. Within the Commission, he became known as the most independent of the group, believing that big communications was as dangerous as big government and big labor.[136]   The Commission's agenda was already loaded with blockbuster issues:

> --the ownership of and the number of domestic communications satellites and what services they would offer;
>
> --the future of digital communications; and
>
> --the entry of the special service common carriers into the market who planned to compete with AT&T.

Burch had his work cut out for him.

---

[134]Murphy, "Federal Regulatory Policy," p. 341.

[135]Lois Vermillion, "Dean Burch: FCC's Pragmatic Boss," Electronics (September 28, 1970), p. 85.

[136]Jimmy Breslin, How the Good Guys Finally Won New York: Ballentine Books, 1976), pp. 132-133.   See note 157, infra.

b. The Office of Telecommunications Policy

The Office of Telecommunications Policy (OTP) was a new addition to the FCC's environment that needs to be noted. In February 1970, President Nixon submitted a reorganization plan to Congress to establish within the Executive Office of the President an Office of Telecommunications Policy with the specific objective of representing the President's views to the FCC and Congress regarding matters such as CATV [cable television], regulation of pay television, assignment of scarce portions of the radio spectrum, "diversification of media ownership. . .and the encouragement of competitive challenges against the Bell Telephone System in specialized communications services."[137] With no objection from Congress, it would become effective within 60 days "equal in rank with the President's staff panels on the economy, science and environment" and it would be headed by Dr. Whitehead.[138] The Executive's Office of Telecommunications Management and Nixon's Task Force were transformed into the OTP in March and given broad powers to shape government policy on computers and communications.[139]

---

[137]Thomas P. Murphy, "Technology and Political Change: The Public Interest Impact of COMSAT," The Review of Politics, 33 (July, 1971), p. 423.

[138]Ibid.

[139]Murphy, "Federal Regulatory Policy," p. 342.

What was the philosophy underlying this new
approach? Was there to be a change in policy resulting
from the OTP's formation? It is easy to understand
that there might be a difference of opinion as to
whether the monopoly regulated should be a public monopoly, a private monopoly, or a hybrid organization such
as COMSAT. The private carriers had been shunted off
the stage in 1961 and 1962 by the Democratic Administration after securing statements from the Eisenhower
Administration favorable to exclusive control of
communications satellites by private industry. However,
the FCC had favored neither COMSAT nor the carriers in
their rulings and there was legislative history that
supported these decisions.

A general review of the White House statements
will clearly show that the Nixon philosophy was not only
intended as supporting greater competition in communications but in other fields (for example, railroads and
aviation) as well.[140] This new office was not intended
to usurp the prerogatives or functions assigned to the
FCC by Congress; it was believed that this new department
and the Commission would cooperate in achieving reforms
in the telecommunications field.[141]

---

[140]Murphy, "Technology and Political Change,"
p. 424.

[141]Taub, "FCC Regulation of Domestic Computer
Communications," p. 953.

c. Congressional Oversight

In addition to its legislative power, Congress has at its disposal a variety of subtle techniques which can influence Commission decisions. One of them is legislative oversight. Standing committees exercise "continuous watchfulness" of the execution of laws by the administrative agencies under their jurisdiction.[142] The standing committees that subpoena the FCC have a significant impact on its activities. "No other Federal agency has been the object of as much vilification and prolonged investigation by Congress," notes Erwin Krasnow, a member of the FCC bar. During the Ninety-First Congress over twenty-five committees and subcommittees attempted to oversee virtually every aspect of the FCC's activities.[143] Congress was interested in DOMSAT.

In 1971 oversight hearings, Congressman Macdonald expressed deep concern over the slow progress that the Commission had been making in the area of domestic satellites.[144] Chairman Burch, in his prepared

---

[142]George B. Galloway, "The Operation of the Legislative Reorganization Act of 1946," American Political Science Review, 45 (1951), pp. 59-60.

[143]Taub, "FCC Regulation of Domestic Computer Communications," pp. 952, 962.

[144]U.S. Congress, House, Subcommittee on Communications and Power, First Session on the Jurisdiction and Activities of the Federal Communications Commission, 92nd Congress, April 29, 1971, p. 1.

statement pointed out:

> Satellites represent an entirely
> new potential for domestic
> communication. Depending on the
> direction and scale of its
> development, domestic satellite
> communications may affect many
> if not all terrestrial systems
> and existing uses of radio and
> cable.
>
> No system can be constructed
> without Commission authorization.
> In this sense, the Commission is
> writing on a clean slate. At the
> same time, however, we are aware
> of the interrelationship between
> any satellite system and existing
> terrestrial facilities. Our
> decisions in this area will
> necessarily have substantial
> economic and technological impact
> all across the common carrier area.
>
> The Commission decided in March
> 1970 that satellites offer suffi-
> cient promise as a mode of domestic
> communications to warrant assign-
> ment of frequencies and use of
> orbital parking spaces.
>
> The first application for a
> domestic satellite system was
> filed on July 30, 1970 and we now
> have pending before us 10
> applications--eight for complete
> systems and two for earth stations
> only.[145]

DOMSAT had been seen by MCI, the specialized

carrier, as advantageous for supplementing their

developing terrestrial system. Four areas of potential

impact [(1) improved network management, (2) heightened

total system reliability, (3) improved earth station

flexibility, and (4) increased broadband capacity]

---

[145]Ibid., pp. 9-10.

were seen.[146] Consequently, MCI Lockheed Satellite Corporation, a joint venture by MCI with the aerospace giant, had announced a week prior to March 15, 1971 [the deadline that the Commission had finally set for DOMSAT construction applications] that it was applying for a permit to construct a $168 million advanced-technology DOMSAT for operation by 1975.[147] This is the root of the story that evolves in Chapter IV.

When Senator Pastore opened oversight hearings of the FCC in February, 1972, his general comments throughout the hearings seemed sympathetic to the complexity of the Commission's task in the face of the different points of view that the public interest can take.[148] Chairman Burch explained that the domestic satellite issue had been delayed by the priority that had been given to the cable television issue. Although open entry appeared favorable, the real problem was trying to determine who should not be permitted into the business.[149]

---

[146]Tom Leming, "An Appraisal of the Role of Satellites in Domestic Communications," presentation before the AIAA 4th Communications Satellite Systems Conference (Washington, D.C.: April 14-16, 1972).

[147]"Lockheed, MCI Team to Propose Domestic Satcom Plan for 1975," Aviation Week and Space Technology (March 18, 1971), p. 186.

[148]U.S. Congress, Senate, Subcommittee on Communications, Overview of the Federal Communications Commission, 92nd Congress, February 1 and 8, 1972, pp. 2, 88-90.

[149]Ibid., p. 98.

Commissioner Johnson, in his last official
appearance before Pastore's subcommittee the following
year, attempted to identify why the Commission
generally had difficulty in developing communications
policy:

> There is much concern these days, as
> well there should be, about the power
> of Congress. The relationship of the
> independent regulatory agencies to the
> Executive Branch and the Congress is a
> useful arena in which to examine that
> power. The idea of the FCC as an
> independent agency established as "an
> arm of Congress" and responsible to it
> is a creed to which the FCC genuflects
> on all appropriate occasions before
> Congressional committees. But it is a
> creed that no one seriously believes
> any longer, because it is not true. . .
> the Executive Branch can and does exer-
> cise control over the FCC.[150]

Additional dialogue went as follows:

> Senator Pastore. The question, Mr.
> Johnson, is why are you not getting
> them [decisions] out? Whose fault
> is it?
> Mr. Johnson. I think it is a variety
> of factors. I think part of it is
> that while we have made some progress
> in terms of a policy planning office--
> we now at least have an office, even
> if we only have one man in it--we,
> basically, have never really had the
> resources to do policy analysis that
> come anywhere close to what Dr.
> Whitehead has, or the Defense Department
> has, or even the FAA, which used to
> have a budget for communications
> research that exceeded the FCC's
> entire budget.[151] We just never

---

[150]U.S. Congress, Senate, Subcommittee on
Communications, Overview of the Federal Communications
Commission, 93rd Congress, February 22, 1973, p. 62.

[151]Burch believes that the rethinking of the

came close to having the number
of professional people we need
as economists and whatnot to help
us with some of these policy
questions.[152]

During the same hearings, Commissioner Richard Wiley

added:

I think the fact that there are
more issues, yet to be resolved is
simply a reflection of the fact
that the technology of the industries
that we regulate is running far
ahead of the policy and the law.[153]

To what extent Congress influenced DOMSAT is

questionable, although certainly in this manner,

some practical check on regulatory action was

undoubtedly being imposed by Congress. Congressional

approval or disapproval of agency action is frequently

intimated and sometimes expressed, either by individual

Congressmen or in committee reports. Such expressions

have some influence on regulatory action, although the

degree of influence varies greatly depending on a

variety of factors. Congress is, of course, in a

position to make its views effectively felt by

regulatory agencies, either by passing controlling

statutes or by pulling on the purse strings of

---

problem, done by Tom Whitehead and a group of White
House experts, significantly influenced the adoption
of an "open skies" policy. Letter from Dean Burch,
Pierson, Ball, and Dowd, Washington, D.C. to Robert
S. Magnant, May 12, 1976.

[152]Overview of the FCC, 1973, pp. 65-66.

[153]Ibid., p. 69.

appropriations. Both of the approaches are highly effective but infrequently invoked.[154]

Other Congressional testimony will be noted throughout the final DOMSAT proceedings in the next section. However, the following points found in a recent House Report are considered worthy of addressing here, for they put the Commission's general problem of policy formulation into perspective. In July 1975, the House Subcommittee on Communications held three days of hearings on Telecommunications Research and Policy Development. Two of the findings of the interim subcommittee report are noteworthy to this review:

> (1) Given the budgetary constraints under which FCC operates, it appears that the Commission will find it extremely difficult to conduct meaningful telecommunications research and policy development internally, although new efforts might result from the recent attempt to enlist the support of the research community.[155]

> (2) What makes the problem of meaningful regulation and policy development even more difficult is that electronic and telecommunications technologies appear to be on a competitive collision course. There is a distinct promise--some would say threat--of the giant in computer technology, IBM, competing with the giant in telephone technology, AT&T,

---

[154]Lee Loevinger, "Regulation and Competition as Alternatives," The Antitrust Bulletin, 11 (1966) p. 128.

[155]U.S. Congress, House, Subcommittee on Communications, Interim Report and Recommended Courses of Action Resulting from the Hearing on Telecommunications Research and Policy Development, 94th Congress, December 1975, p. 11.

and the giant in postal communications,
the U.S. Post Office. All have a stake
in the future of telecommunications
along with COMSAT and the communications
satellite manufacturers, the broadcasters
and the cable operators, among others.[156]

3. The Final Proceedings

Seven years of deliberations, hearings and discussions were slowly drawing to a close. The DOMSAT policy that was finally reached was primarily a product of political reaction to a new invention in a field that was dominated by one private company on the ground and another one in the sky. The policy-making arms of the government perceived, rightly or wrongly, a public distrust for bigness, including government. Under the safe banner of competition as a means to stimulate new ideas and reduced costs, the Commission authorized basically an "open skies" policy as a means to contain bigness.[157]

Burch saw the DOMSAT issue as an example of unnecessary delay. "[W]hen a technology is ready, it shouldn't be kept in the wings," he believed and was inclined to think of the FCC's role in negative terms as "not imposing artificial barriers to technological development." Ironically his favoring of a competitive

---

[156]Ibid., p. 15.

[157]Letter from Mr. Richard P. Gifford, Vice President, Communications Projects, General Electric to Robert S. Magnant, May 7, 1976. Emphasis added.

communications environment put him on the side of the Democrats on the Commission.[158]

By March 1971, with the filings of thirteen applicants before it (five for partial systems), the FCC had some decisions to confront (i.e.--Open entry? Who owns Earth stations? Who can have access?). But after reading the staff's summaries and recommendations, the commissioners found that they could not reach a decision. It is easy enough to see why. A new technology was involved; many conflicting corporate and political interests were involved. The size of the prospective market was uncertain; indeed, since different companies had different notions about the best ways to exploit communication satellites, it might be more appropriate to talk about propspective markets, in the plural.[159]

The staff feared that open entry would not work and that it might end up in monopoly. The main difficulty was the enormous amount of capacity that would come into being if all proposed systems were built; the effect might be that most systems would operate at a heavy loss and only AT&T, which had no problem with a fill factor (because of its ready

---

[158]Vermillion, "Dean Burch: FCC's Pragmatic Boss," p. 85.

[159]John McDonald, "Getting Our Communication Satellite Off the Ground," Fortune, 86 (July, 1972), p. 66; see also the comments by Henson, note 202, infra.

market) would be able to survive.[160]

In October a "Dean Dean" letter from Tom Whitehead stirred the pot:

> There are customers waiting for satellite services and prospective suppliers with capital and the will to offer them on a commercial basis. We see no reason for the government to continue keeping these groups apart. No further studying of applications or enforced commercial arrangements would be as constructive for the using public or for the industry as the prompt opening up of this promising field.[161]

Whitehead made clear not only the Administration's impatience with the Commission to conclude the six-year-old proceeding but also its view that its own open-entry plan should be adopted. Such thinly-veiled criticism of the Commission's pace on DOMSAT seems slightly out of place when White House intervention had stalled progress twice before (the Johnson and Nixon Task Force Studies).[162]

When Senator Pastore opened oversight hearings in February 1972, he stated:

> Ultimately responsibility for the communications of the country rests with Congress; and if the agency we have created to carry out

---

[160] Ibid., p. 122.

[161] "Whitehead Prods FCC on Satellites," Broadcasting (November 1, 1971), p. 38; see also "FCC Expected to Permit Open Satcom Competition," Electronic News (December 13, 1971), p. 28.

[162] Ibid.

the day-to-day implementation of
the policies we have legislated
is having difficulty, we want
to know about it, and help if we
are able. . . . When may we
expect definitive Commission
action on a domestic satellite
policy?[163]

During the subsequent dialogue, Burch raised

what appears to many to be the basic regulatory ques-

tion that was addressed by the Commission; whether

the domestic satellite technology would be given

exclusively to the established carriers or whether

it would be opened up for development by a number

of competitors:[164]

Mr. Burch. . . .The big problem. . .
is the question of disqualification,
not qualification.   In other words,
is there somebody who should not be
in the domestic satellite business?
Senator Pastore.   I do not want to
be misunderstood.   I am merely trying
to get a date   Can we expect an answer
before election day?
Mr. Burch. Yes, sir.
Senator, let me say this.   Even if we
acted tomorrow, the companies involved
will then go back and restructure their
applications and I cannot promise you
there will be a domestic satellite beaming
election results because that--I just do
not know.
Senator Pastore.   But we will have a
decision by then?
Mr. Burch.   Yes, sir.   You will have
a decision.

---

[163]Overview of the FCC, February 1 and 8, 1972,
p. 2.

[164]Letter from Mr. Andrew Margeson, Staff
Economist, House of Representatives.

Senator Baker. Do you have any idea,
Mr. Chairman, or can you tell us
whether that decision will come in
terms of the open entry concept or
not?
Mr. Burch. That will be determined
as part of our determination.
Senator Baker. Before the election?
Mr. Burch. Within 60 days. Yes.
Open entry sounds wonderful, but it
does not solve the question assuming that
open entry that means everybody or that
there are certain people you keep out. That
is the problem.[165]

a. Conflicting Opinions

The Proposed Second Report and Order, prepared

by the Chief of the Common Carrier Bureau and based

on comments received from the eight applicants and

others, was released in March of 1972. This Report

recommended that all applicants found qualified and

proposing similar satellite technology should be

required to consolidate their efforts in a partner-

type relationship.[166] The staff felt that this

grouping of applicants would reduce the required

investment and overhead while leaving each entirely

free to innovate.[167] This fell short of the open-entry

scheme the White House had been advocating since

January 1970. Commission officials indicated that,

in view of the extensive analysis that the staff had

---

[165] Overview of the FCC, p. 98.

[166] 34 FCC 2d 38.

[167] Taub, "FCC Regulation of Domestic Computer
Communications," p. 981.

written to support its position, the staff's position
might be difficult to alter even though some Commissioners, including Chairman Burch and Richard E.
Wiley, were said to favor a policy closer, though not
identical, to the plan suggested by the White House.
At a press conference, Bureau Chief Strassburg noted,
"We have certain recommendations from Mr. Whitehead
as we have from others. I'm not here to defend our
proposals against the White House recommendations."[168]

The staff recommendation was designed to balance
the benefits to be obtained from the competition of
an open-entry plan--including the development of new
technologies--against the financial risks of permitting
unrestricted entry at a time when the market for
domestic-satellite service was, in the bureau's view,
limited, though growing. Whitehead's reported reaction
was an intent to seek legislation if the staff's plan
was adopted. He described "limited open entry" as a
euphemism for saying that the Commission will decide
what applicants are approved. "We would like completely open entry," he emphasized.[169]

OTP had no authority to direct the Commission
to follow its lead. Legally, it had no more standing

---

[168]"FCC Staff Splits with OTP over Satellites,"
Broadcasting (March 20, 1972), p. 37.

[169]"Whitehead Flexes OTP's Muscle," Broadcasting
(April 17, 1972).

in a Commission proceeding than any other petitioner.
But it did have the influence of the White House
behind it, and if that was not enough, it could, if
it thought an issue important enough, go to Congress
or to the courts to obtain Commission compliance.

And in saying that OTP would go to Congress in
connection with the satellite matter, Whitehead said
he considered the question an important one, and not
only in its own terms. The form DOMSAT would take
would provide a precedent for other forms of communications. He noted, "We ought to structure it right."[170]
Oral arguments before the Commission were set to begin
on May 1. After two days of testimony, it was still
not clear whether the Commission was moving towards
the position advocated by the Administration or not.
An assortment of arguments had been presented. Justice,
for instance, suggested that, during the initial
phase of domestic satellite system operations, both
COMSAT and AT&T be prohibited from transmitting
television signals. The staff would have gone further
with respect to AT&T and limited it to the carriage

---

[170]Ibid. Richard P. Gifford, General Electric
Vice President, has taken the position that switched
telephone service must be regarded as a "natural
monopoly" and that the long-haul transmission "pipes"
must also be considered "natural monopolies". He
contends, however, that the services provided over these
"pipes" enjoys no such status and recommends that the
ownership be opened to major users as well as service
suppliers. See "Noted on the News," Telecommunications
Reports, 40, No. 39 (September 30, 1974), p. 37.

of its monopoly services—message toll and wide area
telephone service.

The range of options discussed by the Commission
appears to have been quite broad. At one end,
Commissioner Nicholas Johnson was said to have expressed
as his first choice the removal of AT&T and COMSAT
from consideration for satellite business; other
commissioners, however, reportedly appeared to favor
the Justice-OTP approach.[171]

The concern of companies who sought entry into
the new domestic communications satellite field but
feared the consequences of unrestricted entry was
expressed by a number of those who appeared before the
Commission. Michael Bader, counsel for MCI-Lockheed,
said:

> We couldn't afford open entry.
>
> Let qualified applicants in. But put
> some restrictions on so that there
> will be entry by companies other than
> AT&T and COMSAT. Don't give us the
> reward of a license that will be
> worthless if AT&T takes all the
> business. Private line business is
> petty cash to them. But it's life-
> blood to us.[172]

On the other hand, COMSAT's David Acheson warned
that the restrictions the staff has proposed putting on
COMSAT—principally the requirement that it be forced

_____

[171]"Is FCC Moving to Advocacy of Open-Entry
Satellite Plan?" Broadcasting (May 8, 1972), p. 53.

[172]Ibid.

to choose between leasing facilities to AT&T and serving

other customers--would seriously affect its role in

the international field:

> If you tell COMSAT it is limited to
> any market. . .you'll lose a resource
> created by Congress. We ask the
> Commission to reject the restrictive
> policies recommended by the staff
> and to adopt an open-entry policy.[173]

b. Competition Reemphasized

Commissioner Abbott Washburn sees any attempt

at identifying the most significant factor influencing

DOMSAT policy as an invitation towards oversimplifi-

cation:

> . . .the real policy problems are
> always multi-faceted and the
> pressures and voices influencing
> government are always many and
> varied. Problem solving in a
> democracy is never simple. But
> despite its frustrations and delays
> it is still the best method yet
> devised by man.[174]

However, the free-enterprise preferences of most of the

Commissioners did raise the flag of competition once

again and a policy of "multiple entry" for domestic

satellites was adopted; but not without considerable

dissention. When the Commission issues its Second

Report and Order on June 16, 1972, it emphasized that

---

[173]Ibid.

[174]Letter from Commissioner Abbott Washburn,
Federal Communications Commission, to Robert S.
Magnant, June 3, 1976.

the true extent of public benefit was still undeter-
mined.[175] In its attempts to insure effective entry
into DOMSAT, the Commission could not ignore the
economic dominance of AT&T, with its multi-billion
dollar investments and operations, nor could it fail
to consider the technical advantages enjoyed by COMSAT
by virtue of its established experience and expertise.[176]
In view of all the conflicts and complexities involved
in the creation of this new industry, it is not
surprising that the Commission's vote on the Second
Report was four to three, or that the majority expressed
great uncertainty as to how satellite communication
would actually work out in practice in several
different markets.[177]

In ruling for "multiple entry", the Commission
said that it generally agreed with its staff's concern
about AT&T's "strength and dominance", and about cross-
subsidies that might eliminate competition at the
outset; the majority also agreed to limit the relationship between AT&T and COMSAT. But the Commission
disagreed with the staff's effort to solve the
problem of fill by proposing coalitions based on

[175]35 FCC 2d 844. Second Report and Order.
To be referred to as the Second Report.

[176]Michael J. Morrissey and John J. Smith, "FCC
Activities: Domestic Satellites," George Washington Law
Review, 41 (May, 1973), p. 752.

[177]McDonald, "Getting our Communication Satellite Off the Ground," p. 126.

similar technologies. Instead, the Commission
authorized all the qualified parties, acting either
independently or in coalitions, to operate communication satellites. Burch joined Commissioners Wiley
and Charlotte Reid in dissenting to the Second Report.
In his words:

> We fully supported the concept of
> multiple entry (we had a hand in
> its invention) but we could not go
> along with some of the onerous
> conditions placed on AT&T and
> COMSAT on the basis of their past
> successes in other operations.[178]

However, Burch felt that the Commission "would
have been well advised to adopt a posture of 'least
is best,' to build a base from the irreducible marketplace realities (AT&T traffic) and to offer all
applicants a maximum of options." Instead he charged
that the Commission had "violated every one of these
counsels of caution."[179] His concern was with the
Report's two "fatal flaws: it may retard the evolution
of satellite technology, not get it going, and it
may thus withhold realistic benefits to the public."[180]
He felt that the Commission could do better:

---

[178]Dean Burch, "Public Utility Regulation: In
Pursuit of the Public Interest," Public Utilities
Fortnightly, 92 (September 13, 1973), p. 72.

[179]Victor Block, "Burch Slams Commission on
Domestic Satellite Decision," Telephony, 183 (July
24, 1972), p. 12.

[180]Ibid., p. 13.

> I believe that some inhibitors
> were called for as an interim
> measure--to give AT&T's potential
> satellite competitors a chance to
> get started. . .[181]

In the Second Report, COMSAT was required to form a separate corporate subsidiary if it wished to engage in any DOMSAT venture. The Report also prohibited any joint AT&T-COMSAT proposals. These restrictions were based primarily on the fact that AT&T owned 29 percent of COMSAT's stock and had the ability to elect three of COMSAT's 15 directors.[182]

The effective date previously set for the order (July 25) was postponed by the Commission until October, pending statements of intention from each of the applicants (with regard to their filings and intended courses of action). In the meantime, the Second Report became the subject of several petitions for reconsideration filed by AT&T, COMSAT and others and the Commission planned a later meeting to consider the docket again.[183]

On December 22, 1972, the Commission released its final report, a Memorandum Opinion and Order[184]

---

[181]Burch, "Public Utility Regulation," p. 72.

[182]Morrissey and Smith, "The FCC Activities," p. 753.

[183]David C. Acheson, "Domestic Satellite Proceeding--Status Report," Public Utilities Fortnightly, 90 (December 7, 1972), p. 53.

[184]38 FCC 2d 665, Memorandum Opinion and Order. To be referred to as the Final Report.

and ended seven years of deliberations, hearings, and
discussions on domestic satellite service for the U.S.
The determination of the Commission, in its Final Report,
modified the earlier AT&T/COMSAT restrictions; COMSAT
was still required to form the separate corporate
subsidiary in order to engage in DOMSAT ventures, and
AT&T, its initial use of domestic satellites having been
limited to its noncompetitive services, would now be
permitted to openly compete in both competitive and
noncompetitive markets after three years.[185] Here, the
FCC had in mind the problem of preventing cross-subsidy
and the identification of relevant costs, when AT&T
combined its monopoly telephone services and competitive
services in the same facilities.[186] The Final Report
approved a proposal by COMSAT for joint and equal ownership in a restructured MCI Lockheed Satellite (in which
no single owner, such as COMSAT, would control corporate
management decisions) and the COMSAT servicing of AT&T
with its separate subsidiary. AT&T divested itself of
its COMSAT holdings forcing maximum mutual independence
and COMSAT General, the COMSAT subsidiary, was formed.[187]

---

[185]Morrissey and Smith, "The FCC Activities,"
p. 753--"or upon a finding by the Commission that other
specialized-services licensees have achieved substantial
utilization of their satellite capacity, whichever is
earlier." This was an attempt to minimize the effect of
AT&T's monopoly on new competitors with no established
or protected revenue bases. See also 38 FCC 2d 679.

[186]Bernard Strassburg, "New Technology and Old
Institutions," Telecommunications (June, 1974), p. 25.

[187]Morrissey, "The FCC Activities," p. 756.

Although the Commission's decision on the <u>Final</u>
<u>Report</u> was unanimous, the DOMSAT issue is viewed by
others in many ways. Economist Alfred Kahn, the
Chairman of the State of New York Public Service
Commission says:

> In view of what I see as the Bell
> System's primary commitment to
> terrestrial communications modes,
> I can only feel that the introduc-
> tion of competition, or entrusting
> the exploitation of communications
> satellite technology to some non-
> Bell chosen instrument are essential
> if this new technology is to be
> fully exploited. I find myself
> uncomfortable, however, when
> artificial restraints are placed
> on the competition by the Bell
> System itself, since it seems to
> me, in principle, satellites ought
> to be as fully integrated as technology
> requires with the total communications
> network; and putting limitations
> on AT&T's entry into that field,
> or on the uses that it can make of
> the satellites, it seems to me, may
> frustrate the achievement of that
> goal.[188]

The Common Carrier Bureaus Strassburg looked at
the DOMSAT decision in this way:

> Basically we are embarking on a period
> of trial and error to determine what
> the benefits of domestic satellite
> will be and how the economics will
> spread.[189]

Later he noted:

---

[188]Letter from Dr. Alfred E. Kahn, Chairman,
State of New York Public Service Commission, to
Robert S. Magnant, June 16, 1976.

[189]"The DOMSAT Race is Now Wide Open," <u>Busi-</u>
<u>ness Week</u>, September 22, 1973, p. 68.

> Our task as regulators is to see how
> effective we can be in maintaining the
> demarcation between two new areas of
> the communications market: the first
> is the telephone switched network
> service; the second is the competitive
> market. . .[190]

The 50-page order allowed the U.S. to join the U.S.S.R.
and Canada as users of satellites dedicated to domestic
communications. Burch, in a statement concurring with
the FCC report, stated:

> Candidly, covering up the market-place
> and unfurling protective umbrellas are
> abhorent to me in principle--and the
> limitations we have imposed on AT&T's
> initial use of satellite technology
> clearly crossed the line in both re-
> spects. But we are not here dealing
> just with principle; we are in the
> grip of reality, and we must deal with
> it as best we can.[191]

Burch says:

> In retrospect, it seems like a
> fairly simple idea to prefer competi-
> tion to monopoly, but at the time it
> was a rather momentous step. The
> members of the FCC, while I was there,
> were under considerable pressure to
> reject the "open skies" policy but, to
> their credit, were willing to think the
> unthinkable.[192]

c. Backlash to Competition

Almost immediately after the DOMSAT policy

---

[190]"Profile--Bernard Strassburg," Telephone
Interconnect Journal (November, 1973), p. 32.

[191]Michael Sadofsky, ". . .This Proceeding is
Terminated," Telecommunications (January, 1973), p. 21.

[192]Letter from Dean Burch, Washington, D.C.,
to Robert S. Magnant, May 12, 1976.

was finalized, the din of anticompetitive sentiment
coming from the established carriers became more
pronounced. Whether or not the DOMSAT policy of
competition was the straw that broke the camel's back
is hard to say. Perhaps satellite technology was seen
by the established industry as having the greatest
potential market impact. Prior to 1973, the common
carriers had been fairly indifferent to the "so-called
competition". But apparently times and attitudes were
changing.

Shortly after Carterfone, Dr. Harry Trebing of
Michigan State University referred to common carrier
regulation as "The Silent Crisis" and called for a systems
approach to future regulation, one that would recognize
the coexistence of monopoly and competition. His
praise of FCC policies was based on the Commission's
efforts to accommodate the pressures for change by
promoting greater flexibility in the domestic communications market structure. Additionally remarkable
to him was the fact that these policies evolved in a
regulatory framework which is usually accused of
being reactionary and unresponsive to change.[193] But
this is only one viewpoint of the situation. Senator
Philip Hart had offered these perspectives of

---

[193]Harry M. Trebing, "Common Carrier Regulation--
the Silent Crisis," Law and Contemporary Problems, 34
(Durham, North Carolina: Spring, 1969), pp. 325-329.

competition in the communications industries during

this same period:

> Communications is one area--at least--
> where we should not get hung up on the
> perennial argument of whether antitrust
> exists to protect competition or
> competitors. In communications it must
> protect both. . .
>
> The new technologies should be moving
> us toward more, not less competition. . .
>
> Further, the regulatory agencies should
> encourage parallel systems of electronic
> transmission of written material. If
> success is achieved in this effort, then
> competition, not regulation, could
> determine rates.[194]

In 1970, Leland Johnson also raised questions

of appropriate competitive boundaries between the

traditional franchised monopoly and the competitive

portions of the industry. He concluded that given

the present-day and easily projected technological

basis for the industry, the boundaries might reasonably

be drawn between the so-called "switched" and "un-

switched" portions of the nationwide network along

lines previously suggested by President Johnson's Task

Force.[195]

When Strassburg retired at the end of 1973,

the communications industry suspected that the

Commission's thrust to encourage competition with

---

[194]Philip A. Hart, "The Congressional Perspective of Competition in the Communications Industries,"
The Antitrust Bulletin, 13 (Fall, 1968), pp. 973-978.

[195]Johnson, "Technological Advance," p. 208.

AT&T might be blunted. Those hopes were quickly put down with the appointment of the new Bureau Chief, Walter R. Hinchman. Hinchman, originally an engineer from the Department of Commerce laboratories in Boulder, had come to the FCC via the competitive environments of the Johnson Task Force and the OTP. His initial concern was how AT&T itself competed and he directed his attention immediately to the elements of that issue (i.e., fair rates of return, cross-subsidization, economics of scale, etc.). He also took a dim view of the AT&T counter-offensive to stop or overturn the series of Bureau-supported FCC decisions permitting new competition.[196]

Counter-offensive? Yes, that is correct and directed right from the top. AT&T's Chairman John D. deButts is convinced that regulation and competition do not mix. In 1973, he called for a united front in the telephone industry to end "economic experiments" with competition. His philosophy? DeButts was quoted:

> My instinctive reaction to emerging competition matches that of our first president, who declared, 'We have established and organized the business, and we do not propose to have it taken from us.'[197]

[196]"New Chief of the FCC's Common Carrier Bureau Backs Competition in Telecommunications," Electronics (January 24, 1974), p. 31.

[197]"Who Will Supply the Office of the Future?", p. 49.

His message was contaminating and a campaign
of unmatched sophistication was prepared by the AT&T
headquarters to bypass the FCC. At a meeting of
company presidents in November 1973, AT&T Vice President
Paul M. Lund directed the Bell executives to hammer
home to the public that "competition can be all bad
for the telephone subscriber. . .Take the battle to
politics. . ." he declared, ". . .to municipal
offices, state houses, governor's mansions, meetings
of civic clubs, engineering societies, services
organizations. . .probing and maneuvering for
concensus."[198]

What happened to the deButts, who in a 1970
speech said, "If others can make a contribution. . .it
would seem unreasonable to deny them access,"[199] or
the deButts, who later stated:

> . . .our experience of the consequences
> of the competition from the so-called
> specialized common carriers in the
> private line field has been relatively
> limited. Indeed, in a very real sense,
> it might be said that we have had no
> experience in such competition at all.[200]

DeButts justifies his basic change of mind in
competition:

---

[198]Ibid., p. 49.

[199]Ibid.

[200]"Who Says Competition Isn't Good for the
Market-place? Ma Bell, That's Who!" Telephone
Interconnect Journal (October, 1973), p. 20.

> At first we had no experience with it.
> Now that we have had a couple of years
> of experience we know that it causes an
> increase in troubles. And if it con-
> tinued, there would be an impact on
> rates.[201]

Economist Joseph Schumpeter once observed that no monopoly that acts like a monopoly can expect to survive for any length of time. He reached that conclusion not by looking at the economists' static model of monopoly behavior, but through a profound insight into the dynamics of our economic system. By looking at the long run, he saw not competition, but competitions--a whole myriad of forces that could undermine the unwary monopolist. And there is impressive historical evidence to support his contention.[202]

The traditional idea of telephone service has been replaced by the much broader concept of total communications. Total communications means getting the right information to the right place at the right time--and by information is meant either voice, data, or video service, carried by wire, cable, microwave, or satellite.[203]

---

[201]"Who Will Supply the Office of the Future?", p. 50.

[202]Paul H. Henson, Moderator, "Panel on 'Competition in telecommunications'," Proceedings of the Thirteenth Annual Iowa State Regulatory Conference (Ames, Iowa: Iowa State University, May 1974), p. 27. See also note 159, supra. The introduction of the telephone, which undermined message telegraph service, is probably the best example of this.

[203]Earle G. Bellamy, President of the United

It appears that AT&T has fallen victim to the forces of competition and technology, the impact of which it failed to anticipate. Nicholas Johnson believes that AT&T failed to conceptualize itself as in the 'communications' business rather than the telephone business. What was also to have a great impact, as Johnson saw it in 1969, was the fact that "the telephone company has failed to adequately anticipate and prepare for the present and future demand for communications service for computers."[204]

This set the attitudes for today's DOMSAT activity and provided the background for the entrance of the new kid on the block Satellite Business Systems.

. . . .

The multi-faceted world of the FCC has been shown through the example of the DOMSAT issue. Although every issue of Commission policy making is certainly not as dynamic as was that of the satellite, technology will most likely keep the Commission's world just as complex.

During the period of DOMSAT, the pace of technological change prompted the Commission to re-evaluate the natural monopoly thesis of the market. This applied not only to traditional areas where it

States Independent Telephone Association (USITA), quoted in Public Utilities Fortnightly, 81 (February 29, 1968), p. 47.

[204]Murphy, "Federal Regulatory Policy," p. 342.

was prevalent, but also to the new services that were
being brought about by the rapid confluence of computers
and communications. The agency, through a series of
aggressive decisions of which DOMSAT was the last,
injected the serum of competition into the telecommunications industry in an attempt to treat, if not cure,
its regulatory ills.

Without a doubt, both the FCC and the Nixon
Administration moved towards an active policy of
competition. However, the political pressures that
an Executive element like the OTP could promote do
not seem to have impacted the Commission's decision
significantly. The FCC appears to have been influenced
much more by its own past policies, which had become
more visible at the time of the OTP's formation.[205]
The FCC's response supported competition once again.
The primary criticism raised was that its DOMSAT policy
was so long in coming. To some extent this delay can
be justified by the complexity of the issue and the
complications that were introduced by interrelated
factors of technology, politics and market economics.

Burch and the Commission recognized that the
deferral of certain aspects of the decision-making

---

[205]Trebing has reaching similar conclusions on
this point. See Harry M. Trebing, "A Critique of
Regulatory Accommodation to Change," Regulation in
Further Perspective (Cambridge, Massachusetts: Ballinger
Publishing Co., 1974), pp. 41-65.

process to the marketplace was both a good and necessary thing and "the way the Commission ought to
operate." However, the international considerations
of DOMSAT, although they were recognized, did not
attain sufficient visibility in the proceedings to
insure that today's global impact of DOMSAT would be
recognized by the people of this Nation. There is
no doubt that the Commission's objective in DOMSAT
was to establish a regulatory framework which was
intended to bring the benefits of advanced telecommunications technology to the public as soon as possible
and that the Commission, in assuming its active role,
was attempting to insure fair market competition.
But space resources are global and more attention must
still be given to international regulatory considerations
and the role of the ITU in this area.

Jonathan Rose, Deputy Assistant Attorney General
of the Justice Department's Antitrust Division has
recently noted:

> [The] Above 890 [decision] was decided
> by the FCC without the intervention of
> other Federal agencies such as the
> Justice Department. Similarly, the
> FCC's Carterfone ruling. . .and the
> MCI-Specialized Carrier decisions. . .
> came about as the result of FCC
> initiations.[206]

The fact that the Nation's common carriers are a part

---

[206]Jonathan C. Rose, "Common Carrier Regulation
and Antitrust Policy," Communications News (April, 1976),
p. 16.

of the regulated industry only made the roles of competition and the Commission more important.

CHAPTER IV

DOMSAT POLICY TODAY

By 1973 the Commission's DOMSAT ruling was history and its role of regulator was more difficult than ever, primarily as a result of the dynamics of the evolving industry and its technology. There were five major contenders for this new market (or eight, depending on how the partnerships were counted) that the FCC had to regulate.

Reviews of the "DOMSAT game", with listings of all the players, have already been developed in John McDonald's The Game of Business and Michael Kinsley's Outer Space and Inner Sanctums [cited in the previous chapters] and will therefore not be presented here. Nevertheless, reviewing Satellite Business Systems (SBS), one of the game's newest players, provides one vehicle for looking at some of today's trends in technology and for examining the challenges that the FCC's overall competitive policy, which includes DOMSAT, is being subjected to today.

The ALOHA concept of data communications which is also described in this chapter, has provided an alternative transmission medium to the data communications designer. Although "pure ALOHA" is basically an undisciplined use of the capacity of a communications channel, it may, when used with satellites, be one method for extending shared information processing to the general public, from which a variety of beneficial services could be obtained.

SBS is the successor of MCIL Satellite, which was restructured (with COMSAT participation after the final DOMSAT decision) and renamed CML Satellite Corporation. When IBM announced intentions to acquire 55 percent of CML in July 1974 and get into a new business area, screams came from all directions; some factions believed that the move would stifle "competition"! Even the Federal Trade Commission warned of possible anticompetitive effects in a brief filed with the FCC. Actually, this announcement should not have come as too much of a surprise since IBM had been previously involved in a joint effort with COMSAT in 1967, testing the feasibility of using satellites for wideband data transmission between the U.S. and Europe.[1] The Commission turned down IBM's initial request in January, 1975 but qualified its decision by allowing that a joint venture could be approved if it included one or more additional partners, none of whom would own more than 49 percent nor less than 10 percent of

[1]Stuart L. Mathison and Philip M. Walker, Computers and Telecommunications: Issues in Public Policy (Englewood Cliffs, New Jersey: Prentice-Hall, Inc., 1970), p. 9.

the restructured CML.[2]

On September 27, 1975 Aetna Life Insurance announced that it was teaming up with IBM and COMSAT for a one-third interest in CML Satellite, with plans to build a satellite system largely for the transmission of data instead of voice communications and observers predicted that CML's revenues would reach a billion dollars in the early Eighties, provided it received Commission approval to proceed.[3]

Projected data transmission requirements show this market to be extremely promising; it is large and basically undeveloped. This and the IBM/SBS entry have added a sense of urgency to an AT&T-led campaign to minimize the effects of competition. The result is that proposed legislation is now before the Congress to reverse the FCC's competitive policies and petitions are now before the Commission to deny the SBS filing.

A. Trends in Technology

Some observers see SBS's proposed entry into the DOMSAT market to be in response to the increasing requirement for computer communications. Much of the technology of the DOMSAT systems operating or

[2]"Commission Decides on IBM/COMSAT General Joint Venture," Telecommunications Reports, Vol. 41, No. 4 (January 27, 1975), pp. 1-3.

[3]"Open Skies", Barron's (October 6, 1975), p. 9.

planned today is of an "early COMSAT/1960's" vintage,
which does not meet the increasing requirement for
high data rate communication systems by which computers
can converse [the pessimists though see the pending
entry as an IBM effort to dominate the data communications market and enlarge its computer markets]. In
addition, there has been increasing interest in packet
switching, intelligent networks, and distributive
networks--terms which describe the concept of providing
intelligibility to a communications network. Such a
network comprises a number of geographically dispersed
nodes or remote processors, interconnected by one or
more communication channels.[4] Therefore, before
looking at IBM's DOMSAT entrant, it is beneficial
to review some current examples of computer network
techniques, to look at the projected data traffic
volumes for 1980 and consider the role that domestic
satellite systems can play. To say that such ideas
are simple in concept is not to minimize the difficulties of connection, control and programming involved,
but these difficulties are being approached today in
both obvious and ingenious ways.[5]

---

[4]John F. Buckley, "Network Node Criteria,"
Computer Design, 14 (December, 1975), p. 10.

[5]Stanley Winkler, "Computer Communication--the
Quiet Revolution," Computer Communication--Impacts and
Implications (ACM/ICCC, 1972), p. 30.

1. Data Projections

In recent years it has become commonplace for representatives of the computer industry and others to speak very convincingly of the enormous amounts of data that will soon be transmitted via communications lines throughout the U.S., quoting such authoritative sources as AT&T itself for their information. A 1970 study, performed at Stanford Research Institute for the National Aeronautics and Space Administration,[6] shed some light on this subject by addressing the potential demand for "information transfer" in a broad sense. That is, considering the fact that almost anything written, spoken, photographed or otherwise recorded can be transmitted electrically, what might be the maximum potential demand for all such information transfer activities if appropriate means were made available to implement them?

The study first assembled an extensive list of existing or potential information transfer services. These included electronic mail, remote library browsing, checkless society transactions, video-telephone service and so on, as well as conventional services such as telephone, telegraph and network television program distribution. Next, sample services were selected

---

[6] R. W. Hough et al., A Study of Trends in the Demand for Information Transfer (Menlo Park, California: Stanford Research Institute, 1970).

from the list on the basis either that something was
known about the service or that it looked as though
it might become important if it were to become an
established service. An acceptable projection variable
was then determined for each of the selected services.[7]

The final step was to convert all calls, messages, transactions and the like to a common denominator,
bits (the basic unit of information theory used to
describe message content) of information per year, by
applying a conversion factor related to the transfer
mode assumed for each type operation. The result was
a statement of potential information transfer volume,
expressed in bits, for each service. This information
is illustrated in Figure 3.

In an editorial comment, Green and Lucky noted
that this extensive analysis of the present and
future demands for digital communications which
SRI was still the most up-to-date information
available.[8] A recent Department of Commerce, Office
of Telecommunications Report has updated and added
support to this statement.[9] The OT Report used

---

[7]Roger W. Hough, "Future Data Traffic Volume,"
Computer (September/October, 1970), pp. 6-12.

[8]Green and Lucky, Computer Communications, p. 4.

[9]R. L. Gallawa et al., Telecommunications
Alternatives with Emphasis on Optical Waveguide Systems
(Washington, D.C.: U.S. Department of Commerce, OT
Report 75-72, October, 1975). Chapter II of this
report provides an excellent general discussion

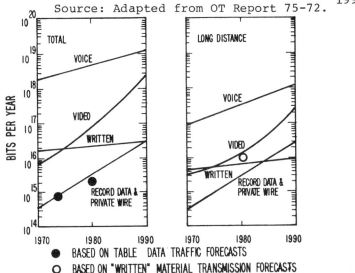

Source: Adapted from OT Report 75-72.

Figure 3.   Projected Information Transfer Volume,
1970-1990.

estimates of growth rates for data transmission

services, such as private wire, teletype (TWX and TELEX)

and telegraph, that were independently derived from

market research tables developed by Datran and

contained in Computers and Telecommunications.[10]   The

data are shown in Table I.   Gallawa et al. have

additionally extracted data from other current Depart-

ment of Commerce reports and used them also to further

update the SRI predictions.   Using electronic mail

as the example, the estimated projected transmission

---

concerning the advantages of digital communications
and the functions forcing the analog to digital
evolution.

[10]Computers and Telecommunications, OECD Informan-
tic Studies 3 (Paris: OECD, 1973), pp. 147-166.

TABLE I

DATA TRAFFIC FORECAST FOR THE UNITED STATES

	1970	1974	1980
Number of Transactions (billions)	14	50	250
Number of calls (billions)	3.7	12	32
Number of data terminals (thousands)	185	800	2,500
Number of termination points (thousands)	84	310	1,000

requirement is approximately 10^{16} (ten million billion) bits of information per year, which correlates with the SRI forecasts (as shown in Figure 3) and reaffirms the basic SRI predictions in order that they may continue to be considered valid for probable communications volume in coming years. The predictions that SBS has submitted to the FCC in support of its pending satellite venture, shed additional light on this area in terms of potential markets and are addressed later in this chapter.

2. Network Developments

There was considerable uncertainty before 1965 about incorporating geostationary communication satellites into the existing telecommunications plant. However, since then satellite channels have been used almost exclusively as replacements for cable or

microwave channels. Only recently does it appear
that the special capabilities of satellite channels
are becoming more widely recognized. These capabilities are largely a result of the computer/communications
research of Dr. Norman Abramson and his staff [which
began in 1968] at the University of Hawaii and some of
the earlier work done by the COMSAT Laboratories in
data transmission.

a. SPADE

SPADE is a system developed for INTELSAT by
the COMSAT Laboratories. SPADE, an acronym for
Single-channel-per-carrier, Pulse code modulation,
multiple-Access, Demand-assigned Equipment, was
developed to utilize the direct multi-point distribution characteristics of satellite communications.
SPADE is appropriate to this discussion since it links
small processors (via satellite) which perform the
signalling and switching functions for the system.[11]

Preassignment of satellite circuits, using full-
time dedicated carriers, provides efficient system
operation for links with heavy traffic. As the number
of circuits per link is decreased, service becomes
increasingly inefficient. One solution is to share
a pool of satellite circuits among Earth stations in

---

[11]Eugene R. Cacciamani, Jr., "The SPADE System
as Applied to Data Communications and Small Earth
Station Operation," COMSAT Technical Review, Vol. 1,
No. 1 (Fall, 1971), pp. 171-182.

common view of the satellite. In the SPADE system,
a chosen satellite RF frequency band is divided on
the basis of assigning a single voice channel per RF
carrier, forming a pool of frequencies for circuits
that can be accessed on demand by any station or
terminal. The system uses a Demand Assignment
Signalling and Switching (DASS) unit for self-assignment
of channels based on continually updated channel
allocation status data provided to a Common Signalling
Channel (CSC).[12]

All signalling between SPADE terminals is
conducted via this single "broadcast" channel. This
feature plus a common signalling format allows
additional terminals to be added, up to the system
maximum, without requiring hardware or operational
modifications to those terminals already in operation.
A Signalling and Switching Processor (SSP) does the
information analysis at each SPADE terminal. The
common signalling channel is a time-shared data channel,
relayed through the satellite, and shared by all SPADE
terminals within the designated community of Earth
terminals. Each operating terminal will transmit
one short data burst of signalling information within
each system time frame. These are received consecutively

[12]Andrew M. Werth, "SPADE: A PCM FDMA Demand
Assignment System for Satellite Communications,"
Proc. Intelsat/IEEE Conf. on Digital Satellite
Communications, 1969, pp. 51-68.

by the satellite and rebroadcast back to all terminals. Thus, each terminal will receive a data burst from all operating terminals during each system time frame. Channel performance parameters are shown in Table II.[13]

TABLE II

COMMON SIGNALLING CHANNEL
PERFORMANCE PARAMETERS

Transmission Bit Rate	---	128,000 bits/sec
Effective Signalling Bit Rate per Terminal	---	960 bits/sec
Bit Error Rate (Maximum)	---	less than 10^{-7}
System Frame Length	---	50 milliseconds
Total No. of Terminals	---	49

Data bursts include bits for carrier recovery, bit timing recovery and unique word synchronization as well as information bits and message error detection bits. One station in the system is designated as the reference station which transmits an additional burst which contains the uniquely identifiable sync word which denotes start-of-frame. Transmission is implemented using a two-phase PSK modem. A BCH Coder-Decoder

[13]G. Dill and N. Shimasaki, "Signalling and Switching for Demand Assignment Satellite Communications," Proc. Intelsat/IEEE Conf. Digital Satellite Communications, 1969, pp. 297-307.

is used to detect up to four errors in a 55 bit
data block.[14]

The SSP was implemented using a small, high
speed 16 bit parallel stored program computer. Since
the functions performed are logical in nature and
highly repetitive, this type unit is ideally suited
for this purpose. Primary operational parameters of
these computers are typically those identified in
Table III. Typical cycle times achieved in existing
SPADE terminals are 180 to 200 microseconds. Since
the SPADE signalling channel uses a time division
multiple access technique, each burst must contain
a sufficient number of bits preceding the information
and bit times between bursts to assure proper synchronization and no burst overlap (a 55 bit preamble and
7 bit times were assigned for synchronization and
quard time respectively).[15]

b. ARPANET

The ARPANET, an experimental communications
system of the Defense Department's Advanced Research
Projects Agency (ARPA), has been extremely successful.
Much has been written on this topic and it is not
intended that this discussion will do any more than

---

[14]Werth, "SPADE: A PCM FDMA Demand Assignment
System for Satellite Communications."

[15]Dill and Shimasaki, "Signalling and Switching for Demand Assignment Satellite Communications."

TABLE III

SIGNALLING AND SWITCHING
PROCESSOR PARAMETERS

° A total of 8192 words of random access memory
(minimum 16 bit words)

° A direct memory access channel (worst case
access time--4 microseconds)

° Program protect capability

° Full cycle programmed memory access of less
than 1 microsecond

° An automatic power failure and restart
capability

---

identify the concept as a forerunner of subsequent

developments. Design objectives for ARPANET were to

develop and test computer-communications techniques

and to ultimately benefit from the resulting resource

sharing. A fully distributed switched message service

was the configuration chosen for the system with the

intent of obtaining greater reliability.[16]

A store and forward system must deal with the

problems of routing, synchronization, error control

and other related issues. To insulate computer centers

from such problems and conversely the communications

network from computer center problems, identical small

processors were chosen to be located at each node of

---

[16]Lawrence Roberts and Barry Wessler, "The ARPA
Network," Computer-Communication Networks (Englewood
Cliffs, New Jersey: Prentice-Hall, 1973), pp. 485-500.

the network, interconnected to form a subnet by leased common-carrier circuits. These Interface Message Processors (called IMP's) connect the computer centers (called Hosts) together with the network, breaking the system design into two parts:

(1) protocol for utilization of the network by the Hosts

(2) implementation of the subnet.[17]

A consideration that later surfaced was how to make this resource available to users without Host facilities or terminal-oriented time-sharing systems. An IMP with flexible terminal handling capability (called TIP), was chosen as the solution, rather than incumbering a nearby Host with composing and translation problems, which an independent terminal user would impose.[18]

Message communications within the subnet are completely autonomous, the average transit time being less than half a second. Transmission is in the form of "packets", each of 1000 bits maximum. Fifteen facilities had been interconnected by February 1971 and the community of users numbered approximately

---

[17]F. E. Heart et al., "The Interface Message Processor for the ARPA Computer Network," AFIPS Conference Proceedings, 40 (1972), pp. 551-567.

[18]S. M. Ornstein et al., "The Terminal IMP for the SRPA Computer Network," AFIPS Conference Proceedings, 40 (1972), pp. 243-254.

2000.[19] By March 1973 the network had grown to 35
nodes. Thus the concept of packet switching for
data/computer communications emerged. If one projects
the growth of computer communication networks like
the ARPANET to a worldwide situation, satellite communication systems become attractive for intercommunications
between widespread geographic areas. The SPADE
system [or the TDMA demand-access system MAT-1] permits
demand assignment of satellite capacity only on
circuit-switched basis for minutes rather than in
small blocks of data or "packets" to a variety of
locations. Several techniques have been proposed and
developed as will be shown.[20] Demand assignment
techniques in general enhance the usefulness of satellite communications networks. They provide advantages
where channel requirements are few and for overflow
traffic for preassigned trunks. Power and bandwidth
efficiencies are also increased.[21] Demand assignment
in smaller elements or "packets" naturally becomes
one of the next logical steps.

---

[19]Roberts and Wessler, "The ARPA Network."
Figure 4 shows the ARPANET one year later.

[20]Lawrence G. Roberts, "Dynamic Allocation of
Satellite Capacity Through Packet Reservations,"
National Computer Conference (1973), pp. 711-716.

[21]J. G. Puente and A. M. Werth, "Demand-
Assignment Service for the INTELSAT Global Network,"
IEEE Spectrum (January, 1971), pp. 59-69.

208

Source: Roberts and Wessler, "The ARPA Network"

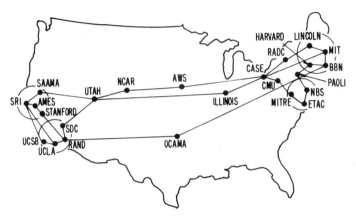

Figure 4.   ARPANET-March 1972

c.   Packet Economics

The predominant force for the past 20 years
in both computer and communications architecture has
been the rapid decrease in computer hardware costs.
Packet switching is strongly dependent on the computing
costs, since computation is used for dynamic bandwidth
allocation, transmission error correcting and reliability through alternative routing.   It is primarily
because the cost of computing has been decreasing far
more rapidly than the price of communications that
such concepts have evolved.

The ARPANET in its present configuration provides a factor of ten or more in cost advantage over
conventional circuit-switched systems.   Available
data can provide some idea of the economics that can be
anticipated in transmitting data via a packet-type of

service. During the month of January 1973 approximately 45 million packets were transmitted by the ARPANET, while its capacity (based on an eight hour day) was about 300 million packets per month.[22]

In March 1973, several contractors were making substantial use of the ARPANET for a majority of their computing resources. An accounting of the utilization at that time and the estimated costs for the network usage and comparable purchased time was developed (see Table IV). Over $2 million a year was being spent on computing resources assessed through the network, resources that would have cost $6 million a year if the network had not existed.

In general, the annual network costs (including the amortization of the message processors) were more than offset by the savings on resources but the significant point is that the network was only using twenty percent of its capacity. Further analysis demonstrated that for a moderate investment in communications, a computing cost reduction factor of three can be achieved by resource sharing in this manner.[23]

[22]Norman Abramson, "Packet Switching with Satellites," National Computer Conference (1973), pp. 695-702.

[23]Lawrence G. Roberts, "Data by the Packet," IEEE Spectrum (February, 1974), pp. 46-51. See also Roy Brunn, "Packet Switching and Satellite Technology," Infosystems, 21 (August, 1974), pp. 33-35.

TABLE IV

COMPUTER RESOURCE USAGE WITHIN ARPANET

User Organization/Activity	Remote Usage	Projected Cost for Replacement
	(thousands)	
U. of Illinois--Parallel processing	$ 360	$1100
NASA Ames--Air foil design	328	570
Rand--Numerical modeling	210	650
Mass. Computer--ILLIAC IV compiler	151	470
Lawrence Livermore--ILLIAC	94	370
Stanford U.--Artificial intelligence	91	180
R.A.D.C.--Text manipulation	81	450
ARPA--On-line management	77	370
Seismic Analysis--Data processing	76	300
Mitre Corp.--File network research	60	240
NBS--Network research	58	200
B.B. & N. Inc.--TENEX support	55	80
Xerox Palo Alto--Computer research	47	100
USC Image Lab--Picture processing	35	70
UCLA--Network measurement	28	90
Systems Control--Signal processing	23	70
U. of C., Santa Barbara-- Network research	22	70
U.S. Air Force--ARPANET management	17	60
Institute for Future-- Teleconferencing	13	40
Miscellaneous--Computer research	192	580
TOTAL	$2018	$6060

Source: Roberts, "Data by the Packet", IEEE Spectrum, February 1974.

Annual remote computer usage costs are based on March 1973 data.

d. Line Control Procedures

Rules have been evolving for the efficient use
of data transmission facilities since J.M.E. Baudot
developed his famous five-unit code more than fifty
years ago. In early code transmission, "start" and
"stop" bits were used to separate characters and to
synchronize the receiving station with the transmitting
station. Synchronous transmission schemes now permit
more information to be passed over a circuit per unit
time because no time is required or lost for the inser-
tion of these signal elements. This discussion only
presents Binary Synchronous Communications (BSC) as
an example of a data link control (DLC) procedure
that can provide for synchronous transmission and the
attachment of multiple terminal devices to a transmission medium. BSC (or Bisync) enables the adapter/
interface equipment to control data flow, maintains
the synchronization between devices, and offers code
flexibility and also transmission efficiency. It
generally conforms to standard line control techniques
of any system that has been designed to deal with
the line errors, addressing, polling and multiplex
problems associated with having an on-line system
with multiple stations.[24]

Communication connections can be simplex

---

[24]IBM, Introduction to Teleprocessing--General
Information, GC20-8095-02 (March, 1973), p. 30.

(unidirectional), half duplex (one way at a time but alternating directions) or full duplex (both ways simultaneously). While the purpose of a DLC is to acquire and maintain synchronization between separate machines, there is usually a higher order user of the communications facility that the DLC ultimately serves. The DLC must act as a conduit for some of the transmitted data, the contents of which should not affect or be affected by the DLC.[25]

BSC transmission is limited to half-duplex over 2-wire or 4-wire private leased or dialed/switched communications channels. All data must be synchronously timed and typically EBCDIC (Extended Binary Coded Decimal Interchange Code) or ASCII (American Standard Code for Information Interchange) is used although an IBM 6-bit Transcode can also be used. The codes comprising the primary control set with BSC are:

> Synchronizing Character (SYN)--is used to establish synchronization. Three SYN characters must precede, and one SYN character must follow, each continuous transmission.
>
> Enquiry (ENQ)--Depending on the state of the transmitting or receiving devices, this is multiple-purpose: solicit the remote device status, request retransmission of a response, and/or indicate an I/O error when transmitting.
>
> Start of Text (STX)--precedes a sequence or block of data characters.

---

[25]J. P. Gray, "Line Control Procedures," Proceedings of the IEEE, 60 (November, 1972), pp. 1301-1303.

Intermediate Block Check (ITB or US or IUS)--
indicates the end of a record in a multiple-
record block.

End of Transmission (ETB)--ends each data
block within a multiple-block transmission.

End of Text (ETX)--is used in lieu of ETB
for the last data block in a transmission.

Data Link Escape (DLE)--when preceding any
character, this alters the meaning of that
character; DLE plus any other character can
be used to create a new control function.

Positive Acknowledgment (ACK Ø or ACK 1)--
are actually character sequences: DLE followed
by the numeric Ø or 1 defines ACK Ø or ACK 1,
respectively. ACK Ø is used to provide a
positive response to all even data blocks;
ACK 1 is a positive response to all odd data
blocks. The first block is considered odd,
the second even, the third odd, and so on.

Negative Acknowledgment (NAK)--is a negative
response to a data block received in error;
it is also used to convey not-ready-to-receive
status to the transmitting device.

End of Transmission (EOT)--terminates the
correct transmission.

Block Check Character (bcc)--performs longitudi-
nal record check.

Peripheral operations available with BSC include

multipoint line control, auto-answer and EBCDIC

transparency. Multipoint line control allows a number

of terminals to operate with a host over a multipoint

communications line. A polling or selection operation

is initiated when the host transmits a 3-character

identification sequence ending in an ENQ. Auto-answer

enables the terminal to automatically answer incoming

calls. Code transparency allows all possible bit

combinations to be used as data. Code sensitivity
that restricts special characters limits the power
of the code being used.[26]

3. The ALOHA Concept

Prior to the ALOHANET, conventional methods
of remote access to a large information processing
system were limited to wire communications--either
private leased or dial-up connections. In some
situations, they were adequate; in others, the
limitations imposed by wire restricted the usefulness
of remote access computing. The use of satellite
systems have only expanded the possibilities of this
concept. The goal of the ALOHA system was to provide
another alternative for the systems designer and to
determine under what circumstances radio communications were preferable to wire for data transmission.

The general availability of wire systems is one
of the obvious reasons for its widespread use in
present day computer-communications systems (although
in many parts of the world reliable high quality
wire networks are not available!). One must remember,
though, that the technology that spawned the voice/wire
networks was one designed for analog signals. This in
itself limits the digital/data transmission capabilities

---

[26] John E. Buckley, "IBM Protocols-Part 1: BSC,"
Computer Design, 14 (January, 1975), pp. 12, 14, 18.

possible and presents a number of drawbacks in the
transmission of binary data.

Data transmitted in a time-shared computer system
comes in a sequence of bursts with extremely long
periods of silence between the bursts. If several
consoles can be placed in close proximity to each
other, multiplexing and data concentration may
alleviate this difficulty. When this is not feasible,
the user may find that his major costs arise from
communication rather than computation and that his
communication system is being used at less than one
percent of its capacity.[27]

a. Pure ALOHA

When the designer of a computer-communication
system is freed from the constraints imposed by the
use of common carrier communications, a number of new
possibilities present themselves. The ALOHANET
uses a radio link. The existing computer-communications
network uses two 24,000 bit-per-second channels in the
UHF band. The system employs message switching
techniques similar to the ARPANET with a novel form
of random-access radio channel multiplexing.

The central computer of the ALOHANET, an IBM
370/158 (an IBM 360/65 prior to December 1974), is
linked to the radio channels by a small interface

---

[27]Norman Abramson, "The ALOHA System--Another
Alternative for Computer Communications," AFIPS, 37
(1970), pp. 281-285. See Figure 5.

216
Source: Abramson, "The ALOHA System"

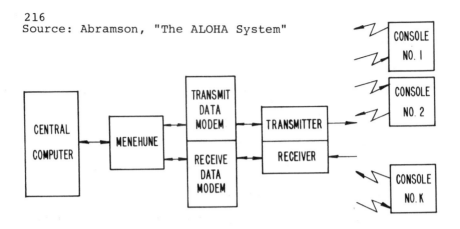

Figure 5. The ALOHA System

computer (whose design is based on the ARPANET IMP)
that has been dubbed MENEHUNE, a legendary Hawaiian
elf. The MENEHUNE is an HP 2115A with a 16-bit word
size, a 1 microsecond cycle time and 8000 words of
core storage.[28]

The ALOHANET has been assigned two 100KHz
channels (407.350 MHz and 413.475 MHz), one for data
from the MENEHUNE and the other for data from the
remote consoles. From the MENEHUNE to the consoles
is no problem since the MENEHUNE can control the
transmitter and buffer messages for the different
consoles. The queues can be ordered according to any
given priority scheme and then transmitted sequentially.
The system presently operates on a first-in, first-out

[28]R. Binder et al., "ALOHA Packet Braodcasting--
A Retrospect," National Computer Conference (1975), pp.
203-215.

basis.

Messages from the consoles are not as easily multiplexed. If standard orthogonal multiplex techniques are employed, the channel would have to be divided into a large number of low-speed channels, each assigned to a particular console, whether it was active or not. Such schemes lead to the same sort of inefficiencies found in wire. The problem could even be partly solved by a system of central control or by a variety of polling techniques. However, ALOHANET uses packets in a common high-speed data channel.[29]

b. Random Packets

The random access method employed by the ALOHA system is based on the use of cyclic error detecting codes. Packets consist of a fixed length of 704 bits (80 8-bit characters plus 32 identification and control bits and 32 parity bits for error detecting) and are transmitted in 30 milliseconds at 9600 bps). Each subscriber transmits packets to the MENEHUNE over the single high data rate channel in a completely unsynchronized (user to user) manner. The transmitting console waits a given amount of time for acknowledgment. Only if a packet is received without error by the

[29] Norman Abramson, "The ALOHA System," Computer Communications Networks (Englewood Cliffs, New Jersey: Prentice-Hall, Inc., 1973).

MENEHUNE does an acknowledgment occur. If none is received, the packet is retransmitted.[30] Since all users access the same channel in 30 millisecond bursts, each automatically multiplexes their data into that channel at the time it's transmitted. The multiplexing is accomplished between the transmitting antenna at each station and the receiving antenna at the central station. One might say that "the medium is the multiplexor."[31]

It is assumed that all error patterns are equally likely. Thus the probability that a given error pattern will not be detected by the error code is 2^{-32} or approximately 10^{-9}. A transmitted packet can be received incorrectly because of two different types of errors: (1) random noise errors and (2) errors caused by interference with a packet transmitted by another console. The former is not considered a serious problem. The interference error is of importance only when a large number of users try to use the single channel and will limit the number of users and amount of data which can be transmitted.[32] Further analysis of ALOHA and its protocol considerations can be found

[30]Abramson, "The ALOHA System--Another Alternative for Computer Communications."

[31]Abramson, "Packet Switching with Satellites."

[32]Abramson, "The ALOHA System--Another Alternative for Computer Communications."

in Appendix C.

c. Satellite Channels

It was previously believed that a satellite system would be of no earthly use [a pun of former FCC Chairman Rosel Hyde] if it could not be connected with terrestrial facilities such as the telephone system. The following is an excellent example of how space technology has done just this and how it has expanded upon the scope of an existing application. A 50 kilobit INTELSAT channel is now being used to link the ALOHA system to the ARPANET and it could easily link additional nodes into the ARPANET at each of the 16 earth stations that have access to the Pacific satellite. For almost a century circuit switching has dominated the design of communications networks. With the higher speed and lower cost of modern computers, packet communications are competitive.

Rather than using satellite channels only as circuit paths, the broadcasting nature of satellites offers two additional unique properties to packet switching. First, not only the broadcasting nature, but the bilateral broadcasting nature of satellites offers certain advantages over normal point-to-point systems. In other words, consider the use of a single channel (like ALOHA) for broadcasting into by transmitters at all ground stations rather than the normal single-transmitter idea of broadcasting. The

second property is that of information feedback. With
a satellite system each ground station has the
capability of transmitting data packets via the
satellite addressed to any other station, but all ground
stations receive each packet, _including the ground_
station that transmitted it, approximately one quarter
second later. With pure ALOHA it was necessary to
provide packet interference information to the sender
in the form of positive acknowledgment. But now, since
each sender can listen to his own packet being retransmitted by the satellite, such information is not
necessary. Thus more efficient use of negative
acknowledgment schemes in conjunction with packet
numbering is feasible for such a system.[33]

Cost trends are rapidly changing with the introduction of domestic satellite communications. If cost
trends follow initial international estimates (see
Table V), the projection of cost performance for
domestic satellites will be very close to that of
computers. The SBS system will take advantage of high
frequency (12-14 GHz) satellite technology which will
permit direct interconnection to the satellite with
very small Earth stations and eliminate the lower limit
of communications costs presently imposed by terrestrial
interconnection.

---

[33]Abramson, "Packet Switching with Satellites."

TABLE V

COST ESTIMATES FOR INTELSAT
COMMUNICATION SATELLITES

IN-TEL-SAT	Usage Year	Number of Circuits	Life-time years	Total Cost	Cost per Circuit per Year
I	1965-67	240	1.5	$ 8.2M	$22,800
II	1967-68	240	3	$ 8.1M	$11,300
III	1968-71	1,200	5	$10.5M	$ 1,800
IV	1971-78	6,000	7	$26.0M	$ 600
V*	1978-85	100,000	10	$28.5M	$ 30

*Estimated   Source: Roberts, "Data by the Packet"

Because ALOHA channels operate in a burst mode
with a duty cycle significantly less than one, the
average power of the channel can be well below the
peak power, just as the average data rate is below
the peak data rate. In initial studies, throughput
analysis was only compared to conventional point-to-
point channels of the same peak power. More recent
analyses have compared channels of the same average
power.[34] Such analysis is of interest in the case of
a satellite information system employing thousands of
small Earth stations. The fundamental limitation in
the down link is the average power available in the

---

[34]Norman Abramson, "Satellite Packet Broadcasting
to Very Small Earth Stations," DCEC Rept. TN-38-75
(Reston, Virginia: September, 1975), 22 pp.

transponder. The results show that in the limit of large numbers of small Earth stations, ALOHA through-put approaches 100 percent of the point-to-point capacity. Multiple access and complete connectivity can be obtained at no sacrifice in average throughput. Higher power satellites (higher peak power while average power is kept constant) permits the small earth stations to use smaller antennas and simpler receivers and modems than is necessary for conventional systems.

Kleinrock and Lam did a model analysis of the performance of a slotted satellite system for packet switching with traffic from many small users (Model I) and for background traffic with one large user (Model II). In the case of Model I, the limiting throughput of the channel [1/exp] can be approached fairly closely without an excessive retransmission delay. With Model II, it was shown that it is possible to increase throughput rather significantly.[35] A single large user can transmit data at a significant percentage of the total channel data rate, thus allowing use of the channel at rates well above the limit of 37 percent obtained when all users have the same message rate. This capability is important for

---

[35]Leonard Kleinrock and Simon S. Lam, "Packet Switching in a Slotted Satellite Channel," Proceed-ings, National Computer Conference (1973), pp. 703-710.

a computer network consisting of many interactive terminal users and a small number of users who send large but infrequent files over the channel.[36]

It is worthwhile noting that another scheme is currently being investigated for packet-switching systems in which the propagation delay is small compared to the slot time. In such systems it may be advantageous for a user to "listen before trans-mitting" in order to determine channel use. Such systems are referred to as "carrier-sense" systems. For satellite communications this small delay/slot time ratio may be found when the capacity of the channel is rather small (approximately 1200 bps for purposes of this discussion), but it should be recognized that this condition is directly related to packet size. In a ground radio environment, a 50 kilobit channel with packets on the order of 100 or 1000 bits lend themselves nicely to carrier-sense techniques. All these tech-niques have complexity/performance trade-offs.[37]

A novel proposal considers the use of a single transponder in a domestic satellite system to provide a public-packet switched data communication service. One INTELSAT IV transponder could easily provide a

---

[36]Abramson, "Packet Switching with Satellites."

[37]Kleinrock and Lam, "Packet Switching in a Slotted Satellite Channel."

data rate of 10 Mbps (the proposed SBS system is to carry 41 Mbps per transponder). Assuming 100 Earth stations, each with small communications controllers, and burst data rates of 10 megabits, the capacity of such a system (in terms of interactive alphanumeric terminals) would be about 100,000 active users. Another interesting point is that the average power in a satellite transponder limits a channel. However, the satellite will only transmit power when it is relaying a packet so when its operation is in a lightly loaded condition, its duty cycle will be small and the average power used low.[38]

In February 1975, COMSAT filed with the FCC for authority to install and operate satellite interface message processor (SIMP) equipment at its Etam, West Virginia Earth station (on a two-year experimental basis in conjunction with single-channel-per-carrier equipment) to provide satellite packet switching to the ARPA Network. Service would initially be between the United States and the United Kingdom.[39] Information on the results to date indicates that the initial strides made in developing this service

---

[38]Abramson, "Packet Switching with Satellites."

[39]"COMSAT Proposes Two-Year Test of 'Packet' Switching," Telecommunications Reports, 41, No. 6 (February 10, 1975), p. 36.

have been highly successful.[40]

As an aside, it is interesting to note that
the question of "actual" packet switching economies
becomes very complex when satellites are used as
the transmission medium. In terrestrial systems, the
value-added carriers (like Telenet Communication,
who offers packet-switching services by means of a
"commercial ARPANET") take advantage of the small
incremental costs that are available when traffic
loading is increased on trunks that normally carry
intermediate levels of traffic. Routing information
(overhead) is added to the basic message to be
transmitted and, although actual throughput is
decreased, more efficient use of the trunking capacity
is obtained and the cost of service to the user
becomes more economical because of decreasing incremental
costs. When trunking facilities are provided by
satellite, because of the "bird's" inherent multipoint
distribution characteristic the economic picture becomes
quite different and there are a variety of opinions
that exist over what the "actual economies" are.

Strangely enough, despite these mixed opinions,
an international standard for packet network protocol
was arrived at this spring in Geneva.[41] Although the

---

[40]Personal Interview with Philip M. Walker,
Vice President and General Counsel, Telenet Communications Corporation, July 7, 1976.

[41]This has been accomplished rapidly because

standard, recommended by the Consultative Committee
on International Telephone and Telegraph (CCITT),
must still be approved at a plenary meeting this
fall, this appears to pose no problem.[42] Recommendation X25, as it is known, supports two basic types
of transmission--permanent and switched virtual
calls. Both require a duplex point-to-point synchronous link between the sender and receiver and his
network node. Telenet has already announced that it
will implement the protocol. IBM has indicated that
it also plans to support it but has not yet said how
long it will take to make the necessary changes in
their existing address control scheme--Systems Network
Architecture (SNA).[43]

B.   The IBM Entry--SBS

Armed with the concepts of computer networks,
packet switching and satellite channels, a discussion
of the impact of the SBS filing should now be more

---

basically no international standard of communication
protocol has previously existed. This is a result of
the fact that in the past most data traffic has been
passed over private-line circuits or that routing or
header information has been provided by the dial
network. [I must thank Mr. Thijs de Haas of the
Department of Commerce for helping me to understand
this complex subject.]

[42]"Protocol for Packet Networks: The Question
is Implementation," Datamation (May, 1976), pp. 187-
188.

[43]Ibid.

meaningful to the reader. A detailed technical analysis of satellite system is not intended but rather an appreciation for the driving force of technology and for the issues that have been raised regarding the DOMSAT policy as applied to the IBM entry.

Upon reading the Commission's thirty-six page Memorandum Opinion and Order on Docket No. 20221, the restructuring of the CML Satellite Corporation, there can be no doubt of the profundity of the basic DOMSAT ruling. The factors relating DOMSAT to interconnect, competition, specialized carriers and Computer Inquiry considerations become more obvious. In December 1975, SBS became the latest applicant for a domestic satellite system and the first to file with the FCC for a system in the 12 and 14 GHz frequency bands. This filing contained the first published description of the SBS system design.[44]

Within ninety days, the AT&T-sponsored "Consumer Communications Reform Act of 1976" was introduced into both houses of Congress. It was not just a reaction to the filing; it was a reaction to the basic idea of the IBM entry, a spectre that had been raised almost

---

[44] For a summary of the system description of the SBS filing, see C. Kittiver and F. R. Zitzmann, "The SBS System--An Innovative Domestic Satellite System for Private-Line Networks," presented at the AIAA/CASI Sixth Communication Satellite Systems Conference (Montreal, Canada: April 5, 1976).

228

two years earlier.

1. A Joint Proposal

In August 1972 Joseph H. McConnell, Chairman
of COMSAT, announced that COMSAT had signed a
Memorandum of Understanding with MCI Lockheed Satellite
Corporation to develop a jointly owned multipurpose
DOMSAT system, contingent upon the FCC's approval of
such a joint proposal.[45] After the Commission's
Final Report approved the COMSAT participation, CML
Satellite, an attempt to combine COMSAT's technical
expertise with MCIL's marketing ability, livened up
the competition. CML proposed to use larger and more
sophisticated satellites than any of the other
contenders[46] and the newer untried frequencies (12 and
14 GHz) which would permit satellite signals to be
beamed, without interference, directly to rooftop
satellite terminals, avoiding "the costly dependency
on interconnections." As Kenneth Crandell, development and planning director put it, "Our motto is:
'don't fight the interconnection problem, avoid it.'"[47]
But CML had other problems. MCI and Lockheed, both

_____

[45]"COMSAT at the Tenth Anniversary of the
Satellite Act," Public Utilities Fortnightly, 90
(September 28, 1972), p. 40.

[46]"The 'DOMSAT' Race is Now Wide Open,"
Business Week, September 22, 1973, p. 70.

[47]"DOMSAT a Year Later: Tight Race," Electronics
(June 21, 1973), p. 72.

of which were having financial difficulties, were looking for buyers for their interests--being unable to make the necessary large capital investments needed.[48]

In a move that surprised both the computer and communications industries, IBM announced on July 3, 1974, that it had agreed to take over fifty-five percent of CML, joining with COMSAT in buying up the Lockheed and MCI interests for a total of $5 million. With its market for computers and data processing systems increasingly dependent on communications links, IBM was prepared to apply its financial and technological muscle to the task of building a new kind of domestic telecommunications network.[49] It thus became the first major communications user with no previous stake in the industry to invest in satellite communications.[50] "Any way you look at it," noted Commission economist Dr. Manley R. Irwin, "IBM's entry has to be considered a major fork in the road."[51]

---

[48]"What Launched IBM into Satellites," _Business Week_, July 13, 1974, pp. 24-25. A recall of seven Earth station applications in February 1974 had been described as "housekeeping" actions by CML.

[49]Ibid., p. 25.

[50]Michael E. Kinsley, _Outer Space and Inner Sanctums_ (New York: John Wiley and Sons, 1976), p. 191.

[51]"Who Will Supply the Office of the Future?" _Business Week_, July 27, 1974, p. 45.

In a joint statement, IBM's chairman Frank T. Cary and COMSAT's president Joseph V. Charyk said, "By joining technical capabilities and experience, we believe we can make a substantial contribution to the development of satellite communications."[52] Sebastian A. Lasher of the White House Office of Telecommunications Policy (and now a consultant to FCC Commissioner Washburn) had guessed right when he told an International Communications Association Conference in January, 1974:

> We can recall the Kingsburg Commitment in 1913, the establishment of the FCC in 1934, and the ATT-Western Electric consent decree in 1956. It seems to me that the time is ripe again in the mid 1970's for this '20-year itch' to manifest itself again. The next five years may be critical for this is a period where the opportunities of change seem to outweigh the risks of change in telecommunications.[53]

Although Cary and Charyk agreed, there were others that did not quite see it that way.

Jack Biddle, Executive Director of the Computer Industry Association, complained that if the IBM-COMSAT joint venture were approved it would enable IBM to monopolize the telecommunications business "in the same way it has monopolized the computer business." He

---

[52]"IBM to Invest $3.2M in CML," Electronic News (July 8, 1974), p. 26.

[53]"Who Will Supply the Office of the Future?", p. 50.

further contended that rather than competing, "AT&T and IBM will simply divide up the market."[54]

Testifying before Senator Hart's Antitrust and Monopoly Subcommittee, Royden C. Sanders, Jr., president of Sanders Associates, Inc. noted:

> Domestic satellites are the key to low-cost communications. A properly implemented switched satellite system providing neutral or transparent interconnections to all users, with no built-in bias toward one equipment supplier, would be very beneficial to the American public and the industries which supply it.
>
> . . .technology exists today that would enable IBM to simply bypass much of the local telephone plants now operated in urban areas by AT&T for business communications by the use of a very small rooftop antenna that communicates directly with the satellite.[55]

However, he warned that those viewing IBM's entry as a panacea for the AT&T monopoly problem were making a catastrophic mistake for IBM's dominance of all elements of a distributed system would make it impossible for meaningful competition to arise.[56] He recommended that the IBM/CML acquisition be denied

---

[54]"IBM Too Big for a Satellite Venture?", Datamation (August, 1974), p. 99.

[55]U.S. Congress, Senate, Subcommittee on Antitrust and Monopoly, Hearings on the Industrial Reorganization Act, S. 1167, Part 7--the Computer Industry, July 23-26, 1974, pp. 5436-5448. Emphasis added. This issue was raised again in September, 1974 by the Computer Industry Association.

[56]Ibid., p. 5438.

because of the potential for market foreclosure and anticompetitive maneuvering.[57]   MCI and Lockheed were ready to sell but the Commission's blessing would have to be obtained first. A petition was filed on July 15, 1974 with the Commission and Docket No. 20221 was opened.[58]

2. The CML Decision

While IBM was saying little about its proposed system, it did note that it would "be different from the first generation systems proposed by the other entrants." It also acknowledged that it would be "a digital satellite transmission system for integrated voice, image and data service, including high-speed data transmission on a multipoint-network basis."[59] In support of the joint petition, CML, IBM, COMSAT and COMSAT General claimed that the financial resources of COMSAT General and IBM would provide assurance in sustaining CML through both the high risk/high cost development stage and later periods when continued long-range viability "will depend on its ability to meet the competition of existing broad-based

---

[57]Ibid., p. 5447.

[58]See Memorandum Opinion and Order, Petition for Approval of Changes in Corporate Structure of CML Satellite Corp., Docket No. 20221, 51 FCC 2d 14.

[59]"IBM Plan: Individual Earth Stations," Electronics (November 14, 1974), p. 67.

communications companies."[60]

Surprisingly AT&T was playing it markedly cool, in sharp contrast to its determined opposition to terrestrial competition. It noted that it had no objection to the proposed change in ownership in CML but reserved the right to address the "public interest questions" it expected to be in CML's formal applications.[61]

Of the 17 parties who provided comments in response to the public notice issued on the joint petition filing, most noteable were the Federal Trade Commission (FTC) and the Computer Industry Association (CIA). The Justice Department, expressing interest in the proposed acquisition, asked the Commission to delay any decision until the question of any possible antitrust violations was resolved.[62] The FTC stated that the IBM/COMSAT petition:

> could have serious anticompetitive effects on the data processing market and sub-markets, and on the integrated business systems market, particularly as they are enhanced by satellite communications.[63]

---

[60]51 FCC 2d 23.

[61]"IBM Plan," p. 67.

[62]"Heard on the Street", The Wall Street Journal (October 25, 1974), 27:3.

[63]"Trade Commission Opposing Joint Venture," Telecommunications Reports, 40, No. 39 (September 30, 1974), p. 17.

They urged "a full and complete factual and legal inquiry into the matter."[64]

The Computer Industry Association is probably the most fearful and most outspoken of all IBM critics. In the September 1 issue of the CIA newsletter On Line, the fear of a CML "lock-in" under which users would be persuaded to rent everything--central computer systems, remote systems, intelligent terminals and even data communications circuits--from a single supplier at least indirectly was strongly evident.[65] It alleged that the IBM "systems" marketing approach would preclude the use of other than IBM equipment and that since no other domestic satellite entrant would be able to provide such "bundled" service, a large segment of the competitive DOMSAT market would be dominated by IBM/COMSAT.[66]

a. SDLC

The CML DOMSAT was seen by the CIA as the missing link that would integrate IBM's computer systems and IBM's "Carnation" private exchange

---

[64]"FTC Slaps IBM-COMSAT Venture Plan," Electronic News (September 30, 1974), p. 1.

[65]"The Ultimate Lock-In?", Modern Data (June, 1975), p. 26.

[66]51 FCC 2d 21.

equipment (PABX-Model 3750) that was being made

and successfully marketed by IBM in France. Another

IBM development was Synchronous Data Link Control (SDLC),

a communications line protocol that provided for

increased transmission efficiency. This was seen as

a means by which the proposed DOMSAT system could be

designed with a built-in bias for IBM to deal "a blow to

competition in the industry."[67]

By comparing SDLC with its forerunner, BSC,

and considering the objectives of its development

(see Table VI) such myths can be discarded. The

"frame", as shown in Figure 6, is functionally

analogous to the "block" terminology used with BSC.

SDLC is a data link control for serial-by-bit synchro-

nous transmission between buffered stations on a

data transmission link using centralized control.

It is bit-oriented and any receiving error invalidates

the entire transmission.

Generally the frame comprises a maximum of

six field positions; of these two are called flags

(F) and they begin and end each frame (with the bit

configuration 01111110). The (A) field is the

address of the secondary station and is always eight

consecutive bits. The primary station has the central-

ized control. The (C) field, also eight bits, contains

---

[67]"The Ultimate Lock-In?", p. 28.

TABLE VI

SUMMARY OF MAJOR REQUIREMENTS

° Control of the data link should remain with a central station to facilitate loop operation as well
as to simplify error recovery procedures.

° Transmission block length should be independent
of message or record length.

° The DLC should allow straightforward transmission
of any message. It should not be possible for any
bit pattern within a transmission to be mistakenly
construed as a control character.

° The DLC should not impose unnecessary line turn-
arounds.

° Operation on systems with a wide range of line
speeds and propagation delays should be possible.

° The basic DLC structure should be equally applic-
able to half-duplex, duplex, reverse channel, hub,
or loop link configurations.

° A simple form of the DLC should be provided for use
with simple stations, with more complex forms
available for more intelligent stations.

° The amount of redundancy for checking purposes
should be variable.

° A common discipline should be used for recovery
from detected errors in the communications link.

° The addressing and control structures of the DLC
should be open-ended.

° The DLC should minimize the down time of all
elements of the system.

° The DLC should provide a means of obtaining status
information from the various system elements.

Source: R. A. Donnan and J. R. Kersey, "Synchronous
Data Link Control: A Perspective," IBM
Systems Journal, Vol. 13, No. 2. (1974).

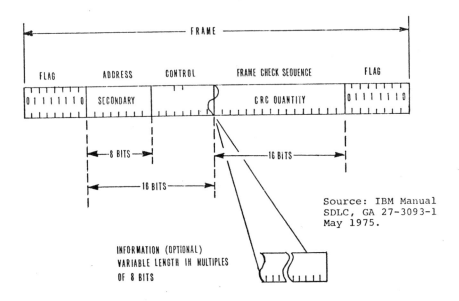

Source: IBM Manual
SDLC, GA 27-3093-1
May 1975.

Figure 6.   The SDLC Frame

control information. It may perform either a command

or a responsive function. The (I) field is the

position of the actual information to be transmitted.

Physical limitations may be imposed on this field by

a terminal but protocol itself does not restrict

format, content or length. The (FCS) field contains

16 bits for cyclic redundancy checking (CRC) used in

frame checking. They represent the complement of a

polynomial remainder calculated on the basis of the

(A), (C) and (I) fields.[68]

---

[68]IBM Synchronous Data Link Control--General
Information, GA27-3093-1, May 1975, pp. 2-5 to 2-9.

Primary advantage of SDLC with respect to the
more familiar BSC procedures is that it exhibits code
structure independence. As a bit-oriented protocol,
operational requirements for peripheral device control
and communications channel control are clearly
separated. Many functions are performed by bit desig-
nation and manipulation. The more traditional protocols
required specific control characters, which sometimes
tended to have multiple interpretations.

From a data reliability standpoint, FCS
requirements encompass multiple types of fields,
such as address, control, and information data, while
BSC error control capabilities are limited to protection of text data only. A major weakness of BSC is
that the response (DLE Ø or 1) must be transmitted
totally unprotected. This can create unrecoverable
situations in the event the response is damaged
during transmission.[69]

One feature of SDLC not possible with BSC is
the ability to initiate and maintain full-duplex data
transmission. Assuming the availability of a properly
configured (4-wire) communications channel, simul-
taneous data transmission is possible between two
data communications devices. This data flow, coupled
with the basic transparency of the protocol with

---

[69]John E. Buckley, "IBM Protocols Part 2: SDLC,"
Computer Design (February, 1975), pp. 14-16.

respect to code structure, suggests a meaningful improvement over the more restrictive BSC procedures.

Actually, in the age of the microprocessor, talk of "built-in biases" seems a bit archaic.[70] Microcomputer converters have been developed for such things as code, protocol and data rate conversion. By applying such devices to interface problems and, for example, using it for SDLC to BSC conversion, the advantages of new protocols or transparency can be obtained.[71]

b. Commission Findings

On November 25, 1974, oral arguments were held. FCC Chairman Richard E. Wiley queried the participants opposing IBM as to what conditions might be appropriate for IBM's entry as a common carrier. Most replies indicated that their objections would be softened if the Commission imposed a number of conditions on entry. Nicholas Katzenbach, IBM's General Counsel, addressed the "split the market" allegation:

> There is no way we will avoid competing
> with AT&T. We would have to be absolutely
> out of our minds--with the Justice Depart-
> ment, Federal Trade Commission and FCC

---

[70]As George Potts, an analyst at Dean Witter and Company noted, "Let's face it, AT&T sets its own standards too." See "Heard on the Street", Wall Street Journal (October 25, 1974).

[71]John E. Buckley, "Microcomputer Converter," Computer Design (February, 1976), pp. 12-14.

looking over our shoulders--to
do so.[72]

The Commission found that the prospect of IBM's
entry held promise for bringing to the public new and
better specialized communications services, thereby
promoting potential realization of DOMSAT policy
objectives. IBM's economic and technological
capabilities, as well as its extensive experience in
the computer and data processing equipment industries,
were seen as strong points. Its knowledge of the needs
of the business customer was also considered to be of
benefit in the development of new and better data
communications services.[73]

The Commission concluded that, among other things,
the IBM entry would create the potential for a new and
different system that was likely to be a strong and
vigorous competitor with AT&T in both the domestic
satellite and specialized services markets.[74] However,
it rejected the proposed corporate ownership structure and ruled that it would entertain any of the
following applications:

(a) "Independent Entry Option."

IBM and COMSAT to enter independently
of each other; COMSAT to have the
option of joining another consortium,

[72]"Questions Suggesting IBM's Entry," Telecommunications Reports, 40, No. 48 (December 2, 1974), pp.
1-2.

[73]51 FCC 2d 26-27.

[74]51 FCC 2d 35.

(b)   "Balanced CML Option."

> COMSAT and IBM to merge but only with
> another partner(s), such that no
> participant would have greater than
> 49% or less than 10% stock ownership.

(c)   "Lease Option."

> COMSAT to provide IBM a space segment
> and to function only as a carrier's
> carrier, unable to offer common carrier
> services directly to the public.[75]

Commissioner Washburn noted in a concurring statement:

> In my judgment the strong technology base
> of IBM and COMSAT, in their respective
> fields, promised an unusual degree of
> public service benefit, should the Commis-
> sion permit them to proceed as proposed.[76]

In a separate statement, Commissioner Glen O. Robinson
also endorsed the decision, believing it to be an
affirmative implementation of the basic DOMSAT
decision.[77]

But the issue was far from dead. Even as IBM
was raising doubt that it would enter the business
under the FCC's conditions, five companies[78] took the
Commission's decision to the U.S. Court of Appeals

---

[75]William Wewer, "IBM, CML Satellite and the
Clayton Act: The FCC's Retreat from Competition in
the Telecommunications Industry," Law and Computer
Technology (March/April, 1975), p. 34.

[76]51 FCC 2d 46.

[77]Ibid.

[78]RCA Global Communications, RCA Alaska Communications, American Satellite Corp., Fairchild Industries,
and the Western Union Telegraph Company.

for the District of Columbia, each of the parties

filing a notice of appeal and a petition for

review.[79] However, the Court dismissed the cases

in February of this year finding "that the order

sought to be reviewed in these cases was not final

agency action ripe for review [no authorized filing

of a restructured CML had been approved by this

docket]." But the court did warn that

> our ruling should not be taken as
> an indication of the court's position
> with respect to the Commission's
> handling and disposition of the
> antitrust issue, particularly as to
> the need for an evidentiary hearing
> to determine the competitive impact
> of the Commission's interlocutory
> ruling.[80]

3. The SBS Filing Today

On December 22, 1975, Satellite Business Systems,

the restructured CML (which is owned 42 1/2 percent each

by IBM and COMSAT and 15 percent by the Aetna Casualty

and Surety Company), submitted its five volume DOMSAT

filing to the Commission for its approval. A systems

design aimed primarily at providing direct point-to-

point, private line circuit replacement had been

dismissed early in the study phase (for the SBS System)

---

[79]"Five Companies Go to Court," Telecommunications Reports, 41, No. 11 (March 17, 1975), p. 5.

[80]The United States Court of Appeals for the District of Columbia Circuit, Order, Nos. 75-1236 through 75-1242, Before: Wright, Tamm and Leventhal, Filed February 23, 1976, George A. Fisher, Clerk.

as not being cost competitive in a market area where
other DOMSAT companies had already announced plans
to offer services. A system providing private line
switched networks (in contrast to point-to-point
services only) with integrated voice, data and image
capability using TDMA with demand assignment of
satellite capacity was chosen instead, having been
determined to have both high growth potential and
near-term demand.[81] Eight operational transponder
channels, each of 54 MHz bandwidth, will have an RF
power output of at least 20 watts. Customers will
purchase capacity to fit their particular needs, but
will also be able to call from a data pool, on demand,
additional bandwidth in 224 kilobit increments.

Because SBS anticipates that the initial users
of its service will be larger enterprises with relatively large communications requirements, it has
examined the five hundred largest United States
industrial corporations, as listed by Fortune magazine,
and the top 50 companies in each of six additional
Fortune categories. From this initial list of 800
companies, SBS selected the 415 companies that
appeared to be the more likely customers for the
initial type of service that SBS proposed to offer.
Demand projections were developed premised upon the

---

[81]Kittiver and Zitzman, "The SBS System," p. 1.

requirements of these companies, to obtain a conservative approximation of the potential demand for the proposed network services. The selection criteria included company revenues, number of employees; present communications usage; installed information processing capability; and geographic dispersion.[82]

Next, in-depth surveys of 16 of these companies, which were believed to be representative of major customer categories, were conducted. This information was then correlated with data obtained from separate sources in order to develop demand projections over a seven year period beginning in 1979. In making these projections, a growth rate of 8 percent per year for voice traffic and 19 percent per year for data traffic was used in obtaining final demand projections for the total number of Earth stations and for total satellite capacity. SBS foresees that a requirement for as many as 7500 such Earth stations could exist by 1986. Using standard interfaces and a totally transparent system, it plans to offer data services from 600 bits per second to 6.312 megabits per second as well as voice and image capabilities to 375 SBS Earth stations.[83]

a.   The Bell Bill

Now that the SBS plan was "out-of-the bag,"

---

[82]Amendment to Operational System Applications, Satellite Business Systems, April 16, 1976, pp. 14-16.

[83]Ibid., pp. 24-25. Based on satellite capacity.

AT&T was less guarded about their plans. As a matter
of fact they were becoming quite outspoken.

Speaking in New York in January, AT&T's deButts
had these corporate comments to share relative to the
competitive policies of the Commission:

> We [at AT&T] believe [that]. . .
> regulated competition. . .is
> adverse to the interest of the
> public.
>
> But it is not for us to decide
> the public interest but rather
> the public itself. . .it is for
> this reason that the telephone
> industry has decided to seek a
> resolution of the issues confronting
> it in the only forum I have long
> felt had the necessary perspective
> to resolve them--the Congress of
> the United States. . .
>
> I do not know whether Congress
> will act or how it will act on the
> legislation that the telephone
> industry--with the support of
> unions representing its employees
> and the support of many regulators--
> will shortly seek to have introduced.[84]

It was a bold bid to stifle competitors. DeButts
was asking Congress to pass legislation that would stop
competition in long-distance services, and permit AT&T
or other traditional carriers to acquire the companies
that would be put out of business. AT&T has suffered
a long series of reversals at the hands of the Commission (which have been upheld in Federal courts), and
by persuading Congress to change the rules, it hopes

---

[84]John D. deButts, "Communications and Public
Policy," Presentation before the Fordham Forum (New
York: January 28, 1976).

to disarm both the Justice Department (in their pending antitrust actions against AT&T) and the FCC.[85] Some believe that the giant monopoly was not truly concerned with the competitive policies of the Commission initially, but that its perception of SBS (with its potential market penetration) rapidly changed that attitude. The basic bills, H.R. 12323 and S. 3192, were introduced into the Congress on March 4 and March 23 respectively. Since that time, according to Congressional staff personnel, over 100 versions of the bill have been introduced into Congress by over 150 sponsors; it seems there is more than a few opinions of what the public interest is. Hearings are not anticipated to begin this Congress and new legislation will have to be reintroduced next session.

Philip N. Whittaker, president of Satellite Business Systems, commenting on the situation, said:

> Satellite Business Systems has given
> the preliminary review to the bills
> recently introduced under the impetus
> of the monopoly carriers. These bills,
> if enacted, would appear to make it

---

[85]"AT&T's Bold Bid to Stifle Competitors," Business Week, March 15, 1976, p. 82. Its most recent setback is in the area of "full competition over the entire range of private line services" for specialized carriers. On July 6, 1976 a three judge panel of the U.S. Court of Appeals for the District of Columbia unanimously affirmed the FCC's policy by upholding the grant of specialized common carrier applications to United States Transmission Systems (USTS), turning down a "narrow" interpretation by AT&T which differentiated between services on the basis of present availability.

virtually impossible for any specialized
carrier to compete with the existing
monopoly communications carriers, unless
the FCC should find that services proposed
by a specialized carrier are 'not like or
similar' to any services provided by a
telephone carrier such as AT&T. This,
at best, would require a difficult and
protracted proceeding before the FCC.

Quite obviously, this legislative effort
seeks to preclude any meaningful competition, and is in direct conflict with the
pro-competitive policies supported by the
FCC, the White House, the Justice Department and most recently by Rep. Macdonald,
Chairman of the House Communications
Subcommittee.[86]

The new industries appear to be game for the

fight.   On May 19, 1976 a group of non-monopoly

telecommunications companies announced the launching

of their joint effort to oppose the proposed legisla-

tion which would eliminate all competition from the

telecommunications market.   The group is called the

Ad Hoc Committee for Competitive Telecommunications

(ACCT).   MCI's Chairman William McGowan, acting as

the spokesman for the group[87] told the press:

The sole purpose of ACCT is to insure
that the Congress--and the consumers of
communications--scrutinize this

---

[86]"AT&T, Competitors Square Off Over Bill to
Repeal Carterfone," Electronic News (April 12, 1976),
p. 50.   The Office of Telecommunications Policy has
recently released a position paper which opposes the
proposed legislation entitled "Competition in Tele-
communications--The Telephone Industry Bill," June, 1976.

[87]Datran, Graphnet, Southern Pacific Communications and USTS comprise the group.   Although SBS and
Telenet are not members of the group, both are
reportedly contributing to it financially.

legislation closely and
carefully.[88]

b. Potential Competition for AT&T

The SBS DOMSAT system, which is not expected
to be in operation until 1979, is called by some "the
first major challenge to American Telephone and
Telegraph's dominance of domestic communications."[89]
Although the direct impact of this application is
some years away, 1979 marks the potential convergence
of several events that are worthy of note. These
include:

    (1) SBS's satellite services will commence.

    (2) IBM's prohibition from entering the data
        services market will end.

    (3) IBM's next generation of new technology
        mainframes will most likely be introduced.[90]

These events have been surfaced in articles forewarning
of the potential threat of IBM, but there is one more
item that should also be included:

    (4) the limitation on AT&T's use of satellites
        to its non-competitive services will
        be removed.

With the inauguration of the services of AT&T's "COMSTAR"
satellite on the Bicentennial, the three-year clock

---

[88]ACCT Press Release, Washington, D. C., May
19, 1976.

[89]"Ma Bell vs. IBM?", Barron's (February 9,
1976), p. 3.

[90]"Market Report-Satellite Business Systems,"
Telecommunications (June, 1976), p. 16.

on AT&T's domestic satellite began and will stop in 1979 unless the Commission acts to extend the limitation.[91]

Petitions to reject the applications of SBS and set the matter for "full evidentiary hearings" or to defer action were submitted to the Commission on June 1, 1976 by nine parties.[92] Common themes ranged from fears of IBM dominance, questions of SBS's compliance with the basic requirements for joint entry laid down by the Commission, and issues of public interest. Taking note of these actions, SBS in a brief statement restated its beliefs that its system will offer significant pro-competitive benefits to communications users and its intent to vigorously pursue its applications.[93] A 311-page response to these comments was filed with the Commission on August 20, 1976 by SBS.

The House Subcommittee on Communications in a recent print has concluded:

> Common carrier regulation in this country is at a critical state. After decades of neglect by federal regulators the FCC began in the mid-1960's to establish the parameters of a meaningful regulatory program.[94]

---

[91]See generally 38 FCC 2d 676-678 and 35 FCC 2d 851-853.

[92]These are American Satellite, the Computer Industry Association, RCA, Western Union, AT&T, GT&E Satellite, Independent Data Communications Manufacturers, RCA Alascom and the State of Hawaii.

[93]"SBS Applications Come Under Strong Attack," Telecommunications Reports, 42, No. 23 (June 7, 1976), pp. 2-4, 27-31.

[94]U.S. Congress, House, Subcommittee on Communications, Agenda for Oversight: Domestic

The report goes on to point out that the decisions made
by the Commission to allow competition with the
established carriers have focused attention on the
inadequacies of FCC regulation (i.e., personnel,
policy planning) without affecting ways of improving
it, noting:

> It would be unfortunate if the FCC's
> current policies of competition were
> to degenerate into a cartelization of
> the market because the Commission
> lacked the resources to do otherwise.[95]

It would also be unfortunate if the benefits of
DOMSAT and the new technology were not realized for
this same reason. Leland Johnson recently addressed
the monopoly/competition issue in the following way:

> [A] particular disconcerting aspect
> of the current controversy is the
> underlying assumption that whoever
> benefits from competition keeps the
> whole amount and whoever loses thereby
> suffers irrevocably. There is little
> recognition of the fact that cost
> savings to one group may be passed on
> at least in part to another group.
> In particular, little consideration
> is given to the possibility that cost
> reductions to the business community
> would be passed on to the consumers--
> including the low income groups whose
> interests everyone seems to want to
> protect.
>
> . . .using rudimentary tools of economic
> theory, one can show that even a
> monopolist will pass a portion of any
> cost reduction to its customers.[96]

Common Carrier Regulations, Subcommittee Print, April
26, 1976, 94th Congress, 2nd Session, p. 26.

[95]Ibid., p. 27.

[96]Leland L. Johnson, "Problems of Regulating

. . . .

At the present time domestic satellite policy
is being strongly influenced by the confrontation
between the advocates of monopoly on the one hand and
the advocates of competition on the other. It appears
that the question before the Commission is not "if"
SBS will be permitted to compete in the industry but
"how" it will enter.

Technological trends, once again, and market
potentials have influenced these advocates and
encouraged IBM to become a major AT&T competitor
and both companies can be expected to structure their
products and services to enhance their ultimate
competitive postures. When the confrontation does
occur many data communications users will be affected
as will the public either directly or indirectly.
There is insufficient evidence to support some contentions that these effects will be adverse. It is more
than likely that the benefits that develop as a result
of this competition for service will far outweigh any
disadvantages recognized.

With an understanding of the background of these
developments, the public can hopefully influence future
FCC policy in an advantageous manner. AT&T has
been generating much "public impact propaganda"

Specialized Telecommunications Common Carriers,"
The Rand Paper Series P-5638, May 1976, pp. 8-9.

252

which should be recognized as such. Information on any of the issues is available from the FCC from the "referee's" point of view. When it comes to the choice between competition and monopoly, their policies have been generally deep rooted and consistent. Even Dean Burch, the conservative Republican, and Nicholas Johnson, perhaps the most liberal Democrat ever to occupy a commissioner's office, voted alike when it came to questions of competition. Although he demeans the Commission, Kinsley also supports competition, noting in the conclusions of his book that without it incentive for innovation disappears and with that goes technological progress.[97]

The Arthur D. Little Company has predicted a world market of telecommunications equipment alone of at least $40 billion a year by 1980 as compared to today's total of only $15 billion a year. Technology will exert pressure for change but it will always be limited by concerns of the marketplace and public policy.[98]

In a 1972 Scientific American dedicated to the theme of communications, Professor Hiroshi Inose of the University of Tokyo wrote:

---

[97]Kinsley, Outer Space and Inner Sanctums, p. 244.

[98]John M. Richardson, "The Technology-Driven Future, the Public Policy-Driven Future or the Market-Driven Future," Communications News (February, 1976), p. 19.

> It is conceivable that a new communi-
> cations network will be built in which
> the transmission, switching and process-
> ing of speech, data and other information
> are all performed digitally. Progress in
> large-scale integrated-circuit technology
> is drastically cutting the cost of
> digital hardware.[99]

Such a system will most likely be first realized

by Satellite Business Systems.

---

[99]Hiroshi Inose, "Communication Networks,"
Scientific American, 227, No. 3 (September, 1972),
p. 128.

254

CONCLUSIONS

Modern communications technology, enhanced
by the computer, its digital technology, and the
advent of the satellite, offers unmatched potential
for enhancing this Nation's telecommunications
systems and promoting innovative services for the
public. The domestic use of communication
satellites gives a new dimension to the systems and
services of today. But this will happen only if the
Nation's telecommunications industry is guided by
relevant laws which are contained within a framework
of technical and economic order. The laws in turn
must stem from a coherent national communications
policy which is based on balanced perspectives of
the future that lie somewhere between academic
optimism, industrial opportunism, and public pessimism.

The regulatory policies of the Federal
Communications Commission, particularly over the past
ten years, have shown an unprecedented responsiveness
to the demands of the public interest and the dynamic
technological environment. Domestic Satellite is
without a doubt one of the finest examples of such
progressive policy making to date. Nicholas Zapple
has noted that such policies have permitted the

regulated communications industry to attain rates of
growth and levels of prosperity that surpass all other
regulated industries.

The Nation's telecommunication industry will
continue to grow and change for the better as a result
of the Commission's competitive policies and the
opportunities and market forces that they generate.
There will always be a need for competition to
accommodate the give and take between the availability
of various communications capabilities and the
applications that people think of for using those
capabilities. But as Clay Whitehead has noted:

> ...the ATT "consumer protection" bill
> shows that the fight for competitive
> and innovative electronic communica-
> tions in the U.S. is far from won.[1]

In a recent address to the International Communications
Association, FCC Chairman Wiley noted that today's
specialized common carriers account for only one-tenth
of one percent of the market while AT&T's _increase_ in
revenues in the competitive services area in 1975
was more than double the total revenues of all competing
suppliers of these services.[2]

----

[1]Letter from Clay T. Whitehead, Santa Monica,
California to Robert S. Magnant, October 21, 1976.

[2]Richard E. Wiley, Address before the International
Communications Association, 29th Annual Conference
(Washington, D.C.: May 3, 1976), pp. 2-3. Total revenues
of the specialized carriers do not exceed $170 million
while the telephone industires revenues are over $4
billion in the competitive market sectors alone.

Professor Joseph Weizenbaum of MIT has raised this thought in his new book, Computer Power and Human Reason concerning the relationship between policy and new technologies:

> Decisions made by the general public
> about emergent technologies depend
> much more on what the public attributes
> to such technologies than on what they
> actually are or can and cannot do. If,
> as it appears to be the case, the public's
> attributions are wildly misconceived, then
> public decisions are bound to be
> misguided and often wrong.[3]

The fact that the Commission has encountered difficulties and opposition to its efforts and that the public is generally unaware of the far-reaching implications of such efforts diminishes neither the laws that guide it nor the agency itself for, in the era of space technology, it has taken in DOMSAT a regulatory giant step.

---

[3]Joseph Weizenbaum, Computer Power and Human Reason (San Francisco, California: W. H. Freeman and Company, 1976), pp. 7-8.

SELECTED BIBLIOGRAPHY

Books

Abramson, Norman, and Kuo, Franklin F., eds. Computer-
Communication Networks. Englewood Cliffs,
New Jersey: Prentice-Hall, Inc., 1973.

Alderson, W.; Terpstra, V.; and Shapiro, J., eds.
Patents and Progress: The Sources of Impact
of Advancing Technology. Homewood, Illinois:
Irwin Publishing, 1965.

Alexandrowicz, Charles H. The Law of Global
Communications. New York: Columbia University
Press, 1971.

Borchardt, Kurt. Structure and Performance of the
U.S. Communications Industry. Boston: Harvard
University Press, 1970.

Clark, Arthur. Voices from the Sky. New York:
Harper and Row, 1965.

Codding, George A., Jr. Broadcasting Without
Barriers. Paris: UNESCO, 1959.

_____. The International Telecommunication
Union. Leiden: E. J. Brill, 1952.

English, H. Edward, ed. Telecommunications for Canada:
An Interface of Business and Government.
Toronto: Methuen Publishing, 1973.

Feldman, N. E., and Kelly, C. M., eds. Communication
Satellites for the 70's. Cambridge, Massachusetts: MIT Press, 1971.

Galloway, Jonathan F. The Politics and Technology
of Satellite Communications. Lexington,
Massachusetts: D.C. Heath and Company, 1972.

Gillmore, Donald M., and Barron, Jerome A. Mass
Communication Law. 2nd ed. St. Paul,
Minnesota: West Publishing Company, 1974.

Green, Paul E., Jr., and Lucky, Robert W., eds.
Computer Communications. New York: IEEE Press,
1975.

Halliwell, B. J., ed. Advanced Communication Systems.
  London: Butterworth, 1974.

Irwin, Manley R. The Telecommunications Industry--
  Integration vs. Competition. New York:
  Praeger Publishing, 1971.

Jones, Erin Bain. Earth Satellite Telecommunications
  Systems and International Law. Austin, Texas:
  The Encino Press, 1970.

Kahn, Alfred E. The Economics of Regulation: Principles and Institutions, Vol. I and II. New
  York: John Wiley and Sons, 1971.

Kinsley, Michael E. Outer Space and Inner Sanctums:
  Government, Business and Satellite Communications. New York: John Wiley and Sons, 1976.

Krasnow, Erwin G., and Longley, Lawrence D. The
  Politics of Broadcast Regulation. New York:
  St. Martin's Press, Inc., 1973.

Martin, James, and Norman, Adrian R. D. The
  Computerized Society. Englewood Cliffs,
  New Jersey: Prentice-Hall, Inc., 1970.

Martin, James. Future Developments in Telecommunications.
  Englewood Cliffs, New Jersey: Prentice-Hall,
  Inc., 1971.

Mathison, Stuart L., and Walker, Philip M. Computers
  and Telecommunications: Issues in Public Policy.
  Englewood Cliffs, New Jersey: Prentice-Hall,
  Inc., 1970.

McDonald, John. The Game of Business. Garden City,
  New York: Doubleday, 1975.

Musolf, Lloyd D. Communications Satellites in
  Political Orbit. San Francisco: Chandler
  Publishing Co., 1968.

Peabody, Robert L.; Berry, Jeffrey M.; Frasure,
  William G.; and Goldman, Jerry. To Enact a
  Law. New York: Praeger Press, 1972.

Phillips, Charles F., Jr., ed. Competition and
  Monopoly in the Domestic Telecommunications
  Industry. Lexington, Virginia: Washington
  and Lee University, 1974.

Sackman, H., and Nie, Norman, eds. The Information Utility and Social Change. Montvale, New Jersey: AFIPS Press, 1970.

Shepherd, William G., and Gies, Thomas G., eds. Regulation in Further Perspective. Cambridge, Massachusetts: Ballinger Publishing Co., 1974.

Trebing, Harry M., ed. Performance Under Regulation. Lansing, Michigan: MSU Public Utilities Studies, 1968.

White, Eston T. Utilities: Electricity, Gas, Tele-communications. Washington, D.C.: Industrial College of the Armed Forces, 1972.

Winkler, Stanley, ed. Computer Communication--Impacts and Implications. ACM/ICCC, 1972.

Articles

Abramson, Norman. "The ALOHA System." Computer Communications Networks. Englewood Cliffs, New Jersey: Prentice-Hall, Inc., 1973.

_____. "The ALOHA System--Another Alternative for Computer Communications." AFIPS, 37 (1970).

_____. "Packet Switching with Satellites." National Computer Conference, 1973.

Abramson, Norman, and Cacciamani, Eugene R., Jr. "Satellites: Not Just a Big Cable in the Sky." IEEE Spectrum (September, 1975).

Acheson, David C. "Domestic Satellite Developments." Public Utilities Fortnightly, 86 (September 24, 1970).

_____. "Domestic Satellite Proceeding--Status Report." Public Utilities Fortnightly, 90 (December 7, 1972).

Averch, Harvey, and Johnson, Leland L. "Behavior of the Firm Under Regulatory Constraint." American Economic Law Review, 52 (1962).

Binder, R.; Abramson, N.; Kuo, F.; Okinawa, A.; and Wax, D. "ALOHA Packet Broadcasting--A Restrospect." National Computer Conference, 1975.

Brunn, Roy. "Packet Switching and Satellite Technology." Infosystems, 21 (August, 1974).

Burch, Dean. "Public Utility Regulation: In Pursuit of the Public Interest." Public Utilities Fortnightly (September, 1973).

Cacciamani, Eugene R., Jr. "The SPADE System as Applied to Data Communications and Small Earth Station Operation." COMSAT Technical Review, 1, No. 1 (Fall, 1971).

Coase, R. H. "The Federal Communications Commission." The Journal of Law and Economics, 2 (October, 1959).

Cohn, Marcus. "The Federal Communications Commission." Rutgers Journal of Computers and Law, 1 (Fall, 1970).

Dill, George D. and Shimasaki, Nobuhiko. "Signalling and Switching for Demand Assignment Satellite Communications." Proceedings of the INTELSAT/ IEEE Conference on Digital Satellite Communications, 1969.

Dingell, John D. "The Role of Spectrum Allocation in Monopoly or Competition in Communications." Antitrust Bulletin, 13 (1968).

Dorff, Ervin K. "Computers and Communications: Complementing Technologies." Computers and Automation (May, 1969).

Gabel, Richard. "The Early Competitive Era in Telephone Communication, 1893-1920." Law and Contemporary Problems, 34. Durham, North Carolina: Duke University, 1969.

Galloway, George B. "The Operation of the Legislative Reorganization Act of 1946." American Political Science Review, 45 (1951).

Geller, Henry. "Competition and Monopoly Policies in Domestic Satellite Communications." The Antitrust Bulletin, 13 (Fall, 1968).

Hart, Philip A. "The Congressional Perspective of Competition in the Communications Industries." The Antitrust Bulletin, 13 (Fall, 1968).

Heart, F. E.; Kalin, R. E.; Ornstein, S. M.; Crowther, W. R.; and Walden, D. C. "The Interface Message Processor for the ARPA Computer Network." 1972 SJCC: AFIPS Conference Proceedings, 40 (1972).

Horowitz, Andrew R., and Cowlan, Bert. "Should People Fight for Satellites." Tele-VISIONS (January/February, 1976).

Hough, Roger W. "Future Data Traffic Volume." Computer (September/October, 1970).

Hurley, Neil P. "Satellite Communications." America. 115 (August 27, 1966).

Johnson, Leland L. "Technological Advance and Market Structure in Domestic Telecommunications." American Economic Association, 60 (May, 1970).

Johnson, Nicholas. "Harnessing Revolution: The Role of Regulation and Competition for the Communications Industries of Tomorrow." The Antitrust Bulletin, 13 (Fall, 1968).

_____. "Why Ma Bell Still Believes in Santa." Saturday Review, March 11, 1972.

Kamien, Morton I., and Schwartz, Nancy L. "Market Structure and Innovation: A Survey." Journal of Economic Literature, 13 (March, 1975).

Kestenbaum, Lionel. "The Limits of a Regulated Monopoly: Telephone Attachments, Interconnections, and Use of Circuits." The Antitrust Bulletin, 13 (1969).

Kleinrock, Leonard, and Lam, Simon S. "Packet Switching in a Slotted Satellite Channel." Proceedings, National Computer Conference, 1973.

Kolb, Burton A. "The Rise and Fall of Public Utilities--An Appraisal of Risk." The Journal of Business, 37 (1964).

Legislative Note. "The Communications Satellite Act of 1962." Harvard Law Review, 76 (1962).

Lessing, Lawrence. "Cinderella in the Sky." Fortune, 76 (October, 1967).

Levin, Harvey J. "Organization and Control of Communications Satellites." University of Pennsylvania Law Review, 113 (January, 1965).

Loevinger, Lee. "Regulation and Competition as Alternatives." The Antitrust Bulletin, 11 (1966).

Mathison, Stuart L., and Walker, Philip M. "Regulatory and Economic Issues of Computer Communications." Proceedings of the IEEE, 60 (November, 1972).

_____. "Specialized Common Carriers." Telephone Engineering and Management (October 15, 1971).

McDonald, John. "Getting our Communication Satellite off the Ground." Fortune, 86 (July, 1972).

Morrissey, Michael J., and Smith, John J. "FCC Activities: Domestic Satellites." George Washington Law Review, 41 (May, 1973).

Moulton, Horace P. "Communications Satellites--The Proposed Communications Satellite Act of 1962." Business Lawyer, 18 (November, 1962).

_____. "Monopoly and Competition Issues Facing the Communications Industries." The Antitrust Bulletin, 13 (Fall, 1968).

Murphy, Thomas P. "Federal Regulatory Policy and Communications Satellites: Investing the Social Dividend." The American Journal of Economics and Sociology, 31 (October, 1972).

_____. "Technology and Political Change: The Public Interest Impact of COMSAT." The Review of Politics, 33 (July, 1971).

Nolan, Herbert. "Moving Business Data is Big Business." Rutgers Journal of Computers and Law, 1 (Fall, 1970).

Notes. "The FCC Computer Inquiry: Interfaces of Competitive and Regulated Markets." Michigan Law Review, 71 (November, 1972).

Ornstein, S. M.; Heart, F. E.; Crowther, W. R.; Rising, H. K.; Russell, S. B.; and Mitchell, A. "The Terminal IMP for the ARPA Computer Network." 1972 SJCC: AFIPS Conference Proceedings, 40 (1972).

Phillips, Charles F., Jr. "Domestic Telecommunications Policy: An Overview." Washington and Lee Law Review, 29 (1972).

Podraczky, Emeric. "Utilization of the Geostationary Satellite Orbit." Telecommunications (January, 1975).

Puente, J. G., and Werth, A. M. "Demand-Assignment Service for the INTELSAT Global Network." IEEE Spectrum (January, 1971).

Riegel, O. W. "Communications by Satellite: The Political Barriers." Quarterly Review of Economics and Business, 11 (1971).

Roberts, Lawrence G. "Data by the Packet." IEEE Spectrum (February, 1974).

_____. "Dynamic Allocation of Satellite Capacity Through Packet Reservation." National Computer Conference, 1973.

Sadofsky, Michael. ". . .This Proceeding is Terminated." Telecommunications (January, 1973).

Schiller, Herbert I. "Communications Satellites: A New Institutional Setting." Bulletin of the Atomic Scientists, 23, No. 4 (April, 1967).

Shayon, Robert Lewis. "Bird Watching." Saturday Review, April 17, 1971.

Shepherd, William G. "The Competitive Margin in Communications." Technological Changes in Regulated Industries. Washington, D.C.: The Brookings Institution, 1971.

Silberman, Charles E. "The Little Bird That Casts A Big Shadow." Fortune, 75 (February, 1969).

Smith, Delbert D. "The Interdependence of Computer and Communications Services and Facilities: A Question of Federal Regulation." University of Pennsylvania Law Review, 117 (April, 1969).

Smythe, Dallas W. "The 'Orbital Parking Slot' Syndrome and Radio Frequency Management." Quarterly Review of Economics and Business, 12 (1972).

Stanley, Kenneth B. "International Telecommunications Industry: Interdependence of Market Structure and Performance Under Regulation." Land Economics (November, 1973).

Strassburg, Bernard. "Communications and Computers: How Shall the Twain Meet?" Public Utilities Fortnightly, 82 (September 12, 1968).

_____. "Competition and Monopoly in the Computer and Data Transmission Industries." The Antitrust Bulletin, 13 (Fall, 1968).

_____. "New Technology and Old Institutions." Telecommunications (June, 1974).

Taub, Barry. "Federal Communications Commission Regulation of Domestic Computer Communications: A Competitive Reformation." Buffalo Law Review, 22 (Spring, 1972).

Trebing, Harry M. "Common Carrier Regulation--The Silent Crisis." Law and Contemporary Problems, 34. Durham, North Carolina: Duke University, Spring, 1969.

Turner, Donald F. "The Scope of Antitrust and Other Economic Regulatory Policies." Harvard Law Review, 82 (1969).

Vermillion, Lois. "Dean Burch: FCC's Pragmatic Boss." Electronics (September 28, 1970).

Walters, Wynn. "Computer Communications: The Start of a Revolution." The Business Quarterly (Winter, 1973).

Werner, Robert L. "A Lawyer Looks at Our Communications Policy." Jurimetrics Journal, 11 (December, 1970).

Werth, Andrew M. "SPADE: A PCM FDMA Demand Assignment System for Satellite Communications." Proc. INTELSAT/IEEE Conference on Digital Satellite Communications, 1969.

Ziegler, Hans K. "Space Communications--A Major Candidate for Commercial Utilization of Space." Advances in the Astronautical Sciences, 28 (1968).

Government Documents

The Communications Act of 1934, with Amendments and Index Thereto. Washington, D.C.: U.S. Government Printing Office.

The Communications Satellite Act of 1962. Pub. L. No.
    87-624, 87th Congress, 2nd Session, August 31,
    1962, 76 Stat. 419.

U.S. Congress. Message from the President of the United
    States. House of Representatives, House Document
    No. 157, 90th Congress, 1st Session, August,
    1967.

U.S. Congress, House, Committee on Government Opera-
    tions. Satellite Communications. H.R. No.
    178, 89th Congress, 1st Session, March 17, 1965.

U.S. Congress, House, Committee on Science and
    Astronautics. Hearings on Communications
    Satellites. 87th Congress, 1st Session, May
    8-10 and July 13, 1961.

_____. Commercial Applications of Space Communica-
    tions Systems. H.R. No. 1279, 87th Congress,
    1st Session, October 11, 1961.

_____. Assessment of Space Communications
    Technology. H.R. No. 859, 91st Congress, 2nd
    Session, March 3, 1970.

U.S. Congress, House, Subcommittee on Communications
    and Power. First Session on the Jurisdiction
    and Activities of the Federal Communications
    Commission. 91st Congress, 1st Session, March
    6, 1969.

_____. First Session on the Jurisdiction and
    Activities of the Federal Communications Commis-
    sion. 92nd Congress, 1st Session, April 29, 1971.

_____. Interim Report and Recommended Courses of
    Action Resulting from the Hearings on Tele-
    communications Research and Policy Development.
    94th Congress, 2nd Session, December, 1975.

_____. Agenda for Oversight: Domestic Common
    Carrier Regulation. Committee Print, 94th
    Congress, 2nd Session, April 26, 1976.

U.S. Congress, Senate, Committee on Aeronautics and
    Space Sciences. Documents on International
    Aspects of the Exploration and Use of Outer
    Space. S. Doc. No. 18, May 9, 1963.

U.S. Congress, Senate, Committee on Commerce. Communi-
    cations Satellite Act of 1962. S.R. No. 1584,
    87th Congress, 2nd Session, June 11, 1962.

_____. Hearings on Communications Satellite
Legislation. 87th Congress, 2nd Session,
April 10-13, 16, 24, and 26, 1962.

U.S. Congress, Senate, Committee on Interstate Commerce.
S.R. No. 781, 73rd Congress, 2nd Session,
April 17, 1934.

U.S. Congress, Senate, Subcommittee on Communications.
Progress Report on Space Communications. Serial
89-78, 87th Congress, 2nd Session, August 10,
17, 18, and 23, 1966.

_____. Overview of the Federal Communications
Commission. 92nd Congress, 2nd Session,
February 1 and 8, 1972.

_____. Overview of the Federal Communications
Commission. 93rd Congress, 1st Session,
February 22, 1973.

U.S. Department of State. Treaties and Other Inter-
national Acts. Series No. 5646, International
Telecommunications Satellite Consortium
(INTELSAT), 1964.

U.S. Federal Communications Commission. Allocation
of Frequencies in the Bands Above 890 MC.
27 FCC 359 (1959).

_____. Authorized Entities and Authorized Users
Under the Communications Satellite Act of 1962.
Docket No. 16058, 4 FCC 2d 421 (1966).

_____. "COMSAT May Furnish Satellite Services
and Channels Only to Other Common Carriers
Except in Unique Circumstances." Public Notice.
4 FCC 2d 12 (1966).

_____. Notice of Inquiry, Establishment of
Domestic Noncommon Carrier Communication
Satellite Facilities by Nongovernmental Entities.
Docket No. 16495, 2 FCC 2d 668 (1966).

_____. Notice of Proposed Rulemaking. Docket No.
16495, 22 FCC 2d 810 (1970).

_____. Petition for Approval of Changes in
Corporate Structure of CML Satellite Corp.
Docket No. 20221, 51 FCC 2d 14.

_____. Regulatory and Policy Problems Presented by the Interdependence of Computer and Communication Services and Facilities. Docket No. 16979, 7 FCC 2d 11 (1966).

_____. Report and Order. Docket No. 16495, 22 FCC 2d 86 (1970).

_____. Second Report and Order. Docket No. 16495, 35 FCC 2d 844 (1972).

_____. Use of the Carterfone Device in Message Toll Telephone Service. Docket No. 16942, 13 FCC 2d 420 (1968).

_____. 38th Annual Report/Fiscal Year 1972. Washington, D.C.: U.S. Government Printing Office.

_____. 39th Annual Report/Fiscal Year 1973. Washington, D.C.: U.S. Government Printing Office.

The White House. Memorandum for the Honorable Dean Burch, Chairman of the Federal Communications Commission. 22 FCC 2d 125 (January 23, 1970).

Periodicals and Newspapers

Aviation Week and Space Technology, 1965-1976. Published weekly by McGraw-Hill Publishing Company, 1221 Avenue of the Americas, New York, New York 10020.

Business Week, 1965-1976. Published weekly by McGraw-Hill Publishing Company, 1221 Avenue of the Americas, New York, New York 10020.

Broadcasting, 1965-1976. The Newsweekly and Broadcasting and Allied Arts. Published by Broadcasting Publications, Inc., 1735 DeSales Street, N.W., Washington, D. C. 20036

Computer Decisions, 1970-1976. Distributed Computing for Management. Published monthly by Hayden Publishing Company, Inc., 50 Essex Street, Rochelle Park, New Jersey 07662.

Computer Design, 1970-1976. The Magazine of Digital Electronics. Published monthly by Computer Design Publishing Corporation, 221 Baker Avenue, Concord, Maine 01742.

Datamation, 1970-1976. A computer industry monthly.
Published by Technical Publishing Company, 1301
Grove Avenue, Barrington, Illinois 60010.

Electronics, 1970-1976. The international magazine of
Electronics Technology. Published bi-weekly by
McGraw-Hill Publishing Company, 1221 Avenue of
the Americas, New York, New York 10020.

Electronic News, 1970-1976. Published weekly by
Fairchild Publications, Inc., 7 East 12th St.,
New York, New York 10003.

IEEE Spectrum, 1968-1976. Published monthly by the
Institute of Electrical and Electronics
Engineers, 345 East 47th Street, New York,
New York 10017.

IEEE Transactions on Communications, 1968-1976. A
publication of the IEEE Communications Society.
Published monthly by the Institute for Electrical
and Electronics Engineers, 345 East 47th Street,
New York, New York 10017.

The New York Times, 1965-1976. Published daily by the
New York Times, 229 West 43rd Street, New York,
New York 10036.

Public Utilities Fortnightly, 1965-1976. Published bi-
weekly by Public Utilities Reports, Inc., Suite
500, 1828 L Street, N.W., Washington, D.C. 20036.

Scientific American, 1965-1976. Published monthly
by Scientific American, Inc., 415 Madison Avenue,
New York, New York 10017

Telecommunications, 1970-1976. An international monthly
on data communications. Published by Horizon
House, 610 Washington Street, Dedham,
Massachusetts 02026.

The Telecommunications Journal, 1969-1973. Monthly
Magazine of the International Telecommunications
Union. CH-1211 Genevre 20, Switzerland.

Telecommunications Reports, 1973-1976. Authoritative
newsweekly of the Telecommunications Field,
1204 National Press Building, Washington, D.C.
20004.

Telephony, 1970-1976. The Journal of the Telephone
Industry. Published weekly by Telephony Publish-
ing Corporation, 53 West Jackson, Chicago,
Illinois 60604.

The Wall Street Journal, 1965-1976. Published daily
        except Saturdays, Sundays and Legal Holidays,
        1701 Page Mill Road, Palo Alto, California
        94304.

                Miscellaneous Sources

Applications of Computer/Telecommunications Systems,
        Organization for Economic Cooperation and
        Development Informantic Studies 8. Paris:
        OECD, 1975.

Codding, George A., Jr. "The U.S. and the ITU in a
        Changing World." OT Special Publication 75-6,
        Department of Commerce, December 1975.

Computers and Telecommunications, Organization for
        Economic Cooperation and Development Informantics
        Studies 3. Paris: OECD, 1973.

Fackelman, Mary P., and Krekel, Kimberly A. "Interna-
        tional Telecommunications Bibliography." OT
        Special Publication 76-7, Department of
        Commerce, March 1976.

Final Report, President's Task Force on Communications
        Policy, December 7, 1968. Washington, D.C.:
        U.S. Government Printing Office, 1969.

Gallawa, R. L.; Bloom, L. R.; Hanson, A. G.; Gray,
        E. M.; and Hull, J. A. Telecommunications
        Alternatives with Emphasis on Optical Wave-
        guide Systems. U.S. Department of Commerce,
        OT Report 75-72, October, 1975.

Hatfield, Dale. "A General Analysis of Domestic
        Satellite Orbit/Spectrum Utilization." U.S.
        Department of Commerce, Office of Telecommuni-
        cations, NTIS PB 207397, December 13, 1971.

Hough, R. W.; Fratessa, Carolyn; Holley, Virginia;
        Samuel, A. H.; and Wells, L. J. A Study of
        Trends in the Demand for Information Transfer.
        Menlo Park, California: Stanford Research
        Institute, 1970.

Hyde, Rosel H. "Space Age Regulation." Presentation
        before the Midwest Association of Railroad
        and Utilities Commissioners. Chicago, Illinois:
        July 7, 1964.

International Telecommunication Union, Joint World
    Plan Committee of the CCIR and CCITT. General
    Plan for the Development of Interregional
    Telecommunication Networks, 1967-1970-1975.
    Geneva: ITU, 1968.

Johnson, Leland L. "Problems of Regulating Specialized
    Telecommunications Common Carrier." The Rand
    Paper Series P-5638, May 1976.

Johnson, Nicholas. "The Capacity to Govern: The Role
    of the FCC in the Development of National
    Policy for Computer Communications." Hopkins-
    Brooking Lecture Series, Computer Communications
    and the Public Interest, Advanced International
    Studies, March 12, 1970.

Kittiver, C., and Zitzman, F. R. "The SBS System--An
    Innovative Domestic Satellite System for
    Private-Line Networks." Presentation before the
    AIAA/CASI Sixth Communication Satellite Systems
    Conference. Montreal, Canada: April 5, 1976.

Laskin, Paul L. Planning for a Planet, An Interna-
    tional Discussion on the Structure of Satellite
    Communications. New York: The Twentieth
    Century Fund, 1971.

Leming, Tom. "An Appraisal of the Role of Satellites
    in Domestic Communications." Presentation before
    the AIAA 4th Communications Satellite Systems
    Conference. Washington, D.C.: April 14-16, 1972.

Melody, William. "Technological Determinism and
    Monopoly Power in Communications." Presentation
    before the American Economic Association.
    New Orleans, Louisiana: December 28, 1971.

The Network Project. Domestic Communications Satellites.
    New York: Its Notebook No. 1, 1972.

Report by the Telecommunication Science Panel of the
    Commerce Technical Advisory Board. "Electro-
    magnetic Spectrum Utilization--The Silent
    Crisis." Washington, D.C.: U.S. Department of
    Commerce, October 1966.

Reports on Selected Topics in Telecommunications. The
    Final Report by the Committee on Telecommunica-
    tions, National Academy of Engineering.
    Washington, D.C.: National Academy of Sciences,
    November, 1968.

Satellite Business Systems. Application of Satellite Business Systems for a Domestic Communications Satellite System, Volumes I, II, and III, December 1975.

Selective List of Studies and Reports on Communication Satellite Projects. Paris: UNESCO, December 1973.

Weil, Gordon L. Communicating by Satellite: An International Discussion. New York: Twentieth Century Fund, 1969.

Wiley, Richard E. Address Before the International Communications Association, 29th Annual Conference. Washington, D.C.: May 3, 1976.

APPENDICES

APPENDIX A

LETTERS, INTERVIEWS OR DOCUMENTS FURNISHED

Norman Abramson, Director
The ALOHA System
University of Hawaii
Honolulu, Hawaii   96822

Walter Adams
Distinguished University Professor
Michigan State University
East Lansing, Michigan   48823

James H. Alleman, Economist
Office of Telecommunications
U.S. Department of Commerce
Boulder, Colorado   80302

Robert S. Black
Exxon Company, U.S.A.
P. O. Box 2180
Houston, Texas   77001

Louis R. Bloom
Office of Telecommunications
U.S. Department of Commerce
Boulder, Colorado   80302

Robert Bottomley
Satellite Business Systems
1750 K Street, N.W.
Washington, D.C.   20006

Dean Burch, Esq.
Pierson, Ball and Dowd
1200 18th Street, N.W.
Washington, D.C.   20036

Carl J. Cangelosi, Esq.
RCA American Communications, Inc.
60 Broad Street
New York, New York   10004

Abram Chayes, Professor
Harvard Law School
Cambridge, Massachusetts   02138

Alexander J. Chisholm, Assistant Vice President
Regulatory Matters
Western Union
1828 L Street, N.W.
Washington, D.C. 20036

R. H. Coase
Clifton R. Musser Professor of Economics
University of Chicago Law School
1111 East 60th Street
Chicago, Illinois 60637

Ms. Gail Crotts
Consumer Assistance Office
Federal Communications Commission
Washington, D.C. 20554

Anthony Cusumano
Director of Traffic
American Broadcasting Company
1330 Avenue of the Americas
New York, New York 10019

Marvin J. Diamond, Esq.
Hogan and Hartson
815 Connecticut Avenue
Washington, D.C. 20006

Wayne Du Bois
AT&T Long Lines
32 Avenue of the Americas
New York, New York 10013

Nathaniel E. Feldman
The Rand Corporation
Santa Monica, California 90406

Joseph R. Fogarty, Esq.
Communications Counsel
United States Senate
Committee on Commerce
Washington, D.C. 20510

Jonathan F. Galloway, Associate Professor
Department of Politics
Lake Forest College
Lake Forest, Illinois 60045

John F. Gerstner
Satellite Business Systems
1750 K Street, N.W.
Washington, D.C. 20006

Richard P. Gifford, Vice President
Communications Projects
General Electric Company
Lynchburg, Virginia 24502

W. J. Gorman, Jr.
Public Relations Director
American Telephone and Telegraph Company
195 Broadway
New York, New York 10007

R. H. Harvey, Manager
Mathematics, Computers and Systems Department
Exxon Corporation
P. O. Box 153
Florham Park, New Jersey 07932

Dale N. Hatfield, Chief
Office of Plans and Policy
Federal Communications Commission
Washington, D.C. 20554

Fred W. Henck, President and Editor
TELECOMMUNICATIONS REPORTS
1204 National Press Building
Washington, D.C. 20045

Andrew R. Horowitz, Co-Director
Public Interest Satellite Association
55 W. 44th Street
New York, New York 10036

Manley R. Irwin, Professor of Economics
The Whittemore School of Business and
  Economics
University of New Hampshire
Durham, New Hampshire 03824

Leland Johnson, Director
Communications Policy Program
The Rand Corporation
Santa Monica, California 90406

Nicholas Johnson
P. O. Box 19101
Washington, D.C. 20036

Alfred E. Kahn, Chairman
New York Public Service Commission
Empire State Plaza
Albany, New York 12226

Dr. Jeffrey Krauss
Office of Plans and Policy
Federal Communications Commission
Washington, D.C. 20554

Ms. Pat Kuhlman
Ad Hoc Committee for Competitive
  Telecommunications
8130 Boone Boulevard
Vienna, Virginia 22180

Sebastian Lasher
Office of Commissioner Washburn
Federal Communications Commission
Washington, D.C. 20554

Robert W. Lucky, Head
Advanced Data Communications Department
Bell Laboratories
Holmdel, New Jersey 07733

Andrew Margeson, Staff Economist
U.S. House of Representatives
Committee on Interstate and Foreign
  Commerce
Washington, D.C. 20515

Stuart G. Meister, Esq.
Regulatory Counsel
American Satellite Corporation
20301 Century Boulevard
Germantown, Maryland 20767

Ralph Metts
International Business Machines
System Communications Division
Gaithersburg, Maryland 20760

Thomas P. Murphy, Professor and Director
Institute for Urban Studies
University of Maryland
College Park, Maryland 20742

Harry Newton
Telecommunications Writer and Consultant
3 Sheridan Square
New York, New York 10014

G. J. Rauchenbach, Director
Congressional and Government Relations
Communications Satellite Corporation
950 L'Eufant Plaza, S.W.
Washington, D.C. 20024

Paul Rodgers, General Counsel
National Association of Regulatory
  Utility Commissioners
1102 Interstate Commerce Commission Building
P. O. Box 684
Washington, D.C. 20044

William B. Rogers
Manager of Data Communications
American Broadcasting Company
1330 Avenue of the Americas
New York, New York 10019

William Schmidt, Jr.
Ground Systems Engineering
Satellite Business Systems
1750 K Street, N.W.
Washington, D.C. 20006

William G. Shepherd
Professor of Economics
University of Michigan
Ann Arbor, Michigan 48104

Kenneth R. Stanley, Economist
Common Carrier Bureau
Federal Communications Commission
Washington, D.C. 20554

Richard Talley
230 Via Anita
Redondo Beach, California 90277

Harry M. Trebing, Director
Institute of Public Utilities
Professor of Economics
Michigan State University
East Lansing, Michigan 48824

Philip M. Walker
Vice President and General Counsel
Telenet Communications Corporation
Washington, D.C. 20036

Commissioner Abbott Washburn
Federal Communications Commission
Washington, D.C. 20554

Harry Watson
Executive Office of the President
Council of Economic Advisors
Washington, D.C. 20506

Gordon L. Weil
Political Intelligence, Inc.
Harpswell, Maine   04079

Clay T. Whitehead, President
Allison Technical Services
1520 Arizona Avenue
Santa Monica, California   90404

Albert D. Wheelon
Vice President and Group Executive
Hughes Aircraft Company
Space and Communications Group
P. O. Box 92919
Worldway Postal Center
Los Angeles, California   90009

Craig F. Williamson
Director of Personnel and Administration
Satellite Business Systems
1750 K Street, N.W.
Washington, D.C.   20006

Nicholas Zapple, Esq.
6518 Valley Court
Falls Church, Virginia   22042

Ms. Cheryl Zegers
Technical Information Specialist
Department of Commerce Library
Boulder, Colorado   80303

APPENDIX B

A CHRONOLOGY OF INDIVIDUALS INTERACTING IN DOMSAT

	1965	1970	1975
The Presidency	John F. Kennedy ○	Lyndon B. Johnson ○	Richard M. Nixon ○	Gerald R. Ford ○
Senate Commo Subcommittee	Senator John O. Pastore - Chairman from 1955 to 1976 ○		
House Commo Subcommittee	Congressman Torbert H. MacDonald - Chairman from 1967 to 1976 ○		
Commission Chairman	Newton Minow ○ E. William Henry ○	Rosel H. Hyde ○ Dean Burch ○	Richard E. Wiley ○
Common Carrier Chief	○ Bernard Strassburg from 1964 to 1973 ○		Walter R. Hinchman ○
Primary DOMSAT Policy Dates	COMSAT Act of 1962 ○ ABC's Proposal ○ Johnson Message ○	Notice of Inquiry ○ Task Force Report ○ Report And Order ○ Flanigan Memorandum ○	Final Report ○ Second Report ○ IBM Entry ○ SBS Filing ○ CML Decision ○ Petitions to Deny ○

APPENDIX C

FURTHER ANALYSIS OF THE ALOHA CONCEPT

For those interested in the details of the
ALOHA concept and its protocol considerations, this
supplementary information has been prepared based
on information contained in several journal articles
prepared by Abramson, Binder, Roberts and others.

Analysis

In Figure 7, "$\underline{t}$" is defined as the duration of
the packet (34 milliseconds including receiver synchronization) and we make the pessimistic assumption
that when overlap occurs neither packet is received
without error. We define a random point process for
$\underline{K}$ active users by focusing our attention on the
starting times of the packets and make a distinction
between packets transmitted for the first time (message
packets) and retransmissions (repetitions). Lambda
($\underline{L}$) is the average rate of occurrence of message
packets from a single user (all users are assumed to
have this identical rate). Thus the random point
process from all active users has an average rate of
occurrence of

$$\underline{r} = \underline{KL}$$

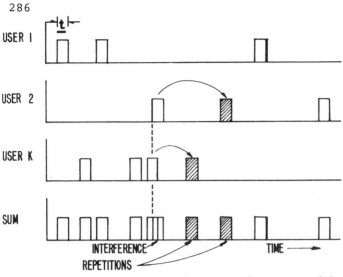

Source: Abramson, "The ALOHA
System"

Figure 7. ALOHA Multiplexing

where r is the average number of message packets per
unit time from K users. If we were able to pack the
messages into the available channel space perfectly
with no space between, then rt, the channel utilization,
would equal 1. Since the channel utilization is
proportional to K users, the objective is to determine
the maximum value of K.

First R is defined as the average number of
message packets plus repetitions per unit time from
K users. R must be greater than r if there are any
repetitions. Rt is thus defined as channel traffic.
It is now assumed that the inter-arrival times of the
point process defined by the start times are independent
and exponential. This is reasonable if the retransmission delay is large compared to t and the number of

retransmissions is not too large (the ratio of the
average time between packets for each user to the
single packet transmission time for the ALOHANET is
about 2000:1).

Under the exponential assumption, the probability
that there will be no starts (of either message packets
or repetitions) in time interval $\underline{T}$ is exp$(-\underline{RT})$. Using
this, a packet will overlap with another packet if
there exists at least one other start point $\underline{t}$ or less
seconds before or after the start of the given packet.
Thus the probability that a given message will be
repeated is

$$1 - \exp(-2\underline{Rt})$$

If we relate $\underline{R}$ (the average number of message packets
plus repetitions) to $\underline{r}$ (the average number of message
packets) we get

$$\underline{R} = \underline{r} + \underline{R}\ [1 - \exp(-2\underline{Rt})]$$

or

$$\underline{rt} = \underline{Rt}\ [\exp(-2\underline{Rt})]$$

Note that the channel utilization (or the capacity of
the random access channel) reaches a maximum value
of 1/2(exp) = 0.184, at which point the traffic on
the channel becomes unstable and the average number of
retransmissions becomes unbounded. The maximum number

of interactive users the system can support can be
found by setting

$$\underline{rt} = \underline{KLt} = 1/2(exp)$$

A conservative estimate for $\underline{L}$ is 1/60 corresponding to
each active user sending a message packet at an
average rate of once a minute. With $\underline{t}$ equal to 34
milliseconds, then

$$K_{MAX} = 324.$$

Bear in mind additionally that while a user is not
active he consumes no channel capacity so that the
total number of users of the system can be a considerably larger number than the 324.[1]

It was later realized that it is possible to
modify the completely unsynchronized use of the ALOHA
channel described in order to increase the channel
capacity. In pure ALOHA each user simply transmits
a packet when ready without any attempt at coordination
with other users, leading to somewhat inefficient
channel utilization. Slotted ALOHA establishes a
time base and each user is required to start his
packets only at certain fixed instants. The channel
is slotted into segments of time equal to the packet

---

[1] Norman Abramson, "The ALOHA System," Computer
Communications Networks (Englewood Cliffs, New Jersey:
Prentice Hall, 1973).

transmission time and users are required to begin
transmissions at the beginning of time slots. The
access is still random in the sense that terminals
transmit into random slots, and if necessary retransmit
after waiting a random number of slots. In this
fashion, if two or more messages conflict they will
overlap completely rather than partially. It has been
shown that the effective capacity of this scheme is
1/exp of the nominal capacity (twice the previous
capacity) using the same assumptions as before.[2]

A third method for using these channels is to
attempt to schedule their use in some direct fashion;
this introduces the notion of a reservation system in
which time slots are reserved for specific users'
transmissions. Every M slots, one slot is subdivided
into V small slots for reservations and acknowledgments.
The remaining M large slots are RESERVED for data
packets. A reservation is a request for from one to
eight RESERVED slots. Both the ALOHA and the RESERVED
technique depend for their efficiency on the total
multi-station traffic rather than individual station
traffic. The reservation system is a factor of three
more efficient than the ALOHA system and for large

---

[2]Norman Abramson, "Packet Switching with Satellites," National Computer Conference, 1973. Figure 8 is a plot of Rt versus rt, for a pure ALOHA channel and a slotted ALOHA channel.

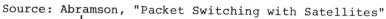

Source: Abramson, "Packet Switching with Satellites"

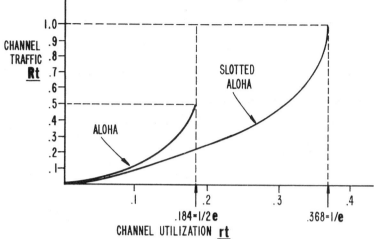

Figure 8. Channel Utilization vs. Channel Traffic

(100 KB) traffic levels achieves almost perfect

channel utilization.[3]

Protocol Considerations

Several of the original choices for the ALOHA

concept have undergone significant changes as a

result of new resources and interfaces or advancements

in theoretical knowledge. Binder, Abramson, Kuo,

Okinawa, and Wax recently updated several aspected of

the concept.

(1) Random access control. The retransmission

strategy used in the random access scheme plays a

central role in the scheme's effectiveness. It can

---

[3]Lawrence G. Roberts, "Dynamic Allocation of
Satellite Capacity through Packet Reservation," National
Computer Conference, 1973.

affect the average delay experienced by users and prevent channel saturation (where the channel becomes filled with retransmissions and the number of successful packets falls to zero). These topics have only been recently quantified in the dissertations of Metcalf at MIT and Lam at UCLA. One approach is to use different retransmission constants at each node to avoid packet conflicts. This results in a priority structure. By simply dividing users into two groups--one transmitting at high power and the other at low power--Metzner notes that another type of hierarchical structure can be established (increasing channel utilization to about 53 percent in the process). Programmable Control Units (PCU's) are another way in which a high degree of systems protocol flexibility can be permitted.[4]

(2) Channel queuing. The MENEHUNE acts as a concentrator for the broadcast channel, queuing waiting traffic when necessary for sequential transmission to user nodes. It is important that the return channel traffic not prevent the prompt return of an ACK to a user and cause unnecessary repetitions. A scheme with an ACK queue, as shown in Figure 9, is

_____

[4]R. Binder, N. Abramson, F. Kuo, A. Okinawa, and D. Wax, "ALOHA Packet Broadcasting--A Retrospect," National Computer Conference Proceedings, 1975, p. 205. see also J. J. Metzner, On Improving Utilization in ALOHA Networks, IEEE Transactions on Communications, April 1976, pp. 447-448.

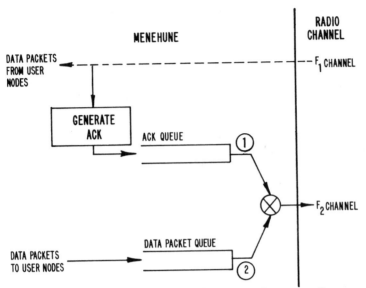

Source: Binder, "ALOHA Packet Broadcasting"

Figure 9. Priority Queues

used so that the ACK's are checked for after each F_2 channel transmission. This guarantees that at most one complete data packet plus any previously queued ACK's will be sent ahead of the next data packet. Hogging of the channel by a few users is also eliminated by queuing. Only one packet per user is allowed on the queue at any one time.[5]

(3) Packet length. The initial use of "half-packets" proved to be a significant source of hardware and software bugs and defeated the "simplified design and construction of the hardware" purpose of fixed-length packets. An end-of-line (EOL--eight zero

[5]Ibid., pp. 206-207.

bits) indicator was used to identify the end of
actual data, which was restricted to 7-bit ASCII.
Formats have now been changed to allow for variable
length packets. An 8-bit count field is used in the
header to indicate the number of 8-bit data bytes in
the packet. This eliminates wasted channel capacity
and the unambiguous detection of the EOL indicator.[6]

(4) Error control. Because of the high
probability of errors at full loading of the random
access channel, reliable error detection is achieved
with two 16-bit parity check words, one following
the header and one following the data. The separate
header check forms the basis for reliable packet
synchronization (discussed below) and accurate
establishment of the packet length and other information prior to processing of the packet data.[7]

(5) Flow control. Complications to the
MENEHUNE flow control processing were caused by the
connection of the ALOHANET to the ARPANET via a 50
kilobit INTELSAT IV satellite path. The quarter
second propagation time and the ARPANET protocol
required a substantial increase in the size of the
MENEHUNE buffer pool and a more complicated queuing
structure. To support broadcast channels, generally

[6]Ibid., p. 207.

[7]Ibid., p. 208.

more than one packet per user must be stored. A large
amount of buffering is required at the receive end of
the link to support continuous display at higher speed
terminals. A 9600 bps terminal requires approximately
a 1000-byte buffer. In general CRT terminal users do
not require continuous output at this rate and a
smaller amount of buffering is in fact used. To
maintain the single-packet-per-user policy for the
channel queue, a separate queue was created for each
user to hold additional packets. The maximum allowed
size for each user queue is adaptive to the user's
terminal rate and buffer pool availability.[8]

Broadcast channel flow control was necessary
since each line (packet) sent to a user node must be
completely displayed before a new line can be received.
This was accomplished by the scheme shown in Figure 10,
in which the control for each user node is centralized
at the MENEHUNE. The latter counts off the required
display time following transmission of each packet to
a user, inhibiting further transmission to that user
until the time is up. To prevent 360 output from
tying up MENEHUNE buffers while packets are being
displayed, a handshaking flow control is used; the
360 sends only one line of output for each user, then
waits for a go-ahead (GA) message with that user's

---

[8]Ibid., p. 210.

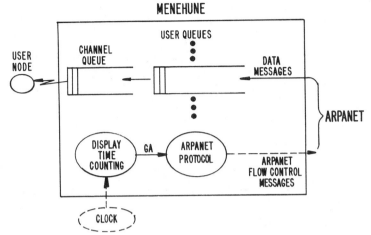

Source: Binder, "ALOHA Packet Broadcasting"

Figure 10. Broadcast Channel Flow Control

address. The GA is sent by the MENEHUNE whenever
a user's display time is up, resulting in at most
one buffer required for each user. Many ARPANET
computers interact with their users full duplex.
Since no explicit flow control was normally provided
for input from users to the MENEHUNE, users were
forced to either interact in a half-duplex mode or
suffer occasional losses of input data. Added buffer
pool capability helps permit full duplex interaction.
If the ARPANET slows down, an excessive amount of
buffers could become queued in the MENEHUNE on behalf
of the user. To prevent buffer hogging, a count of
input queues per user is maintained and when maximums
are reached, arriving packets are discarded and the
user is so notified.[9]

---

[9]Ibid., p. 211.

(6) <u>Synchronization</u>. ALOHANET requires special synchronization techniques in the modem and data terminal equipment. The phase-shift-keying used in the modem design is a bit-synchronous technique and bit synchronization must be performed in the demodulator before packet synchronization can be attempted. The bit-sync detection is designed to provide very low false detection (less than 10^{-6}) and high probability of packet detection. This requires a bit-sync preamble of 90 bits for reliability. By redesigning the phase-lock circuit, this can be reduced to about 10 bits. Present plans are to do away with the bit-sync preamble entirely. Packet synchronization in the data terminal buffer is accomplished by the 16-bit parity word in the packet header. When the parity check routine accepts the header, the packet is assumed to be synchronized. Less than one out of a thousand packets will be lost due to packet sync errors.[10]

---

[10]Ibid., pp. 212-213.